TWAYNE'S WORLD AUTHORS SERIES

A Survey of the World's Literature

Sylvia E. Bowman, Indiana University

GENERAL EDITOR

FRANCE

Maxwell A. Smith, Guerry Professor of French, Emeritus
The University of Chattanooga
Former Visiting Professor in Modern Languages
The Florida State University

EDITOR

Jules Romains

(TWAS 280)

TWAYNE'S WORLD AUTHORS SERIES (TWAS)

*The purpose of TWAS is to survey the major writers—
novelists, dramatists, historians, poets, philosophers, and
critics—of the nations of the world. Among the national
literatures covered are those of Australia, Canada, China,
Eastern Europe, France, Germany, Greece, India, Italy,
Japan, Latin America, the Netherlands, New Zealand,
Poland, Russia, Scandinavia, Spain, and the African
nations, as well as Hebrew, Yiddish, and Latin Classical
literature. This survey is complemented by Twayne's United
States Authors Series and English Authors Series.*

*The intent of each volume in these series is to present
a critical-analytical study of the works of the writer;
to include biographical and historical material that may
be necessary for understanding, appreciation, and critical
appraisal of the writer; and to present all material in clear,
concise English—but not to vitiate the scholarly content
of the work by doing so.*

Jules Romains

DENIS BOAK

University of Calgary

Twayne Publishers, Inc.　　:　:　New York

ISBN 0–8057–2775–2

MANUFACTURED IN THE UNITED STATES OF AMERICA

Acknowledgments

I should like to express my gratitude to the Canada Council, whose generous financial assistance provided invaluable help in the preparation of this study, and to the President and Fellows of Clare Hall, Cambridge, for their hospitality during Summer, 1971. My thanks also go to the staffs of the Library of the University of Calgary and the Bibliothèque Nationale for assistance in obtaining research materials, and to Mrs. Del Lavallée for her help in preparing the typescript. I am also deeply grateful to my wife for her aid and encouragement at all times.

Calgary, October 1972.   D.B.

Preface

At his death, Jules Romains was the doyen of French men of letters. Still actively at work in his mid-eighties, he made several literary reputations for himself: as poet, playwright, and novelist, while in latter years his preferred form was the essay. He became a classic in his own lifetime; several of his plays reached the repertoire of the Comédie Française, while his works, as well as being studied in universities and schools, have been widely diffused all over the world in translation. Yet this popularity was accompanied by an uncompromising emphasis on literary standards, to the extent of evolving rigorous new principles of prosody and embarking on the longest single novel in Western literature.

The difficulties of treating Romains in a study of this type, in the space available, are obvious. The sheer bulk of his literary production necessarily limits critical comment. He published well over a hundred volumes; exactly how many is arguable since various individual books have been republished later, often under a different title. In his study, all Romains's works are discussed, but greater emphasis has been placed on those which seem more significant and likely to survive. Thus an attempt has been made to combine a comprehensive and informative treatment of his work with some depth of judgment. The method used is in the main chronological, bearing in mind that frequently Romains was engaged in major literary projects which overlapped. To divide up a literary career spanning nearly seventy years is inevitably somewhat arbitrary: four main periods have been selected which mark reasonably distinct stages in Romains's development. The first runs from his teens until the outbreak of war in 1914, a traumatic event in his life, as it was to most writers of his generation. During these years, Romains made his reputation, first as a poet, later as a writer of vigorous prose fiction. The second period takes us from 1914 to 1932, when Romains's main energies were expended in the theater, although he also produced a novel trilogy and more poetry. Our third period covers the years 1932 to 1946, which span the publication of *Les Hommes de Bonne Volonté*. In the latter year, Romains returned to France from his wartime exile in North America, was elected to the Académie Française, and began a new stage in his career as a distinguished senior figure in the literary world. This fourth period takes us from 1946 to his death in 1972, during which time Romains produced further novels and a considerable number of essays.

Critical estimates of Romains have varied. There are several reasons for this. Longevity does little in the short term for a literary reputation; far less, certainly, than premature decease. In the last quarter of a century, Romains's work has been overshadowed by the newer generation of Camus and Sartre, whose role in World War II seemed more active than Romains's, and their work therefore more "relevant." The still later generation of *nouveaux romanciers* has turned its back on Romains and the so-called Existentialists alike. He, for his part, never showed himself particularly charitable towards, or even much interested in, younger writers. His very popularity—his sales have run into the millions—has been used as a reason to deny him genuine quality. This is an example of a type of critical snobbery from which envy is scarcely lacking; in general, Romains did not truckle to popular taste—nor did he fail to point this out more than once—but carried his readers with him. And like Victor Hugo, an admired model, he consistently maintained the aesthetic principle that literature should, while preserving its own standards, make the widest popular appeal and not simply cater to a narrow élite. Another criticism of Romains has been that he wrote far too much, and in attempting various different literary genres spread himself too thin. Certainly, any writer with a similar output will be bound to produce uneven work—like Hugo again—and it seems unlikely that most of what Romains wrote after 1946 will in the end add much to his reputation. But we should remember that he was a professional writer, in the fullest sense. Endowed with considerable facility, and indefatigable energy, throughout his career he used his pen not only for purely literary purposes, but also for journalism and lectures. There is nothing wrong with this, and the fact that he produced, say, books of travel impressions, or collected political articles, has no bearing whatsoever on the quality of his novels or poems. His ideal was, indeed, that of the universal man, the *homo plenarius*, Goethe even more than Hugo. This accounts for his wide-ranging literary ambitions and, at the same time, for his desire to make a major scientific discovery, or to play a leading political role. Inevitably, he could not be equally successful in all spheres. However, it seems undeniable that in recent years his reputation as a novelist has overshadowed some of his earlier work, particularly his poetry, whereas a figure like Apollinaire, whose literary production was more concentrated, and a good deal slimmer, no doubt because of an early death, has attracted much more critical interest. The very breadth of Romains's interests will, in the end, nevertheless, be seen as part of the measure of his achievement.

Another obstacle to appreciation of Romains's work is his egoism. As an adolescent, at the outset of his literary career, he seems to have been both shy and sensitive; but these qualities, attractive in youth, become less so if, as the years go on, they harden into pride and touchiness. In any case, modesty was never one of Romains's virtues, though he on occasion boasted of it. Unanimism was accompanied from the start by a good deal of drumbeating, and throughout his career Romains appeared somewhat self-satisfied, even smug. What are we to think of a writer who makes a character in a novel favorably compare one of his own plays with Molière? Frequently, legitimate pride has congealed into simple vanity, to the point of flawing certain of his works, while a tendency towards didacticism, perhaps natural in one trained as a teacher, in later years turned into pontification. Perhaps also he seemed to appreciate the things of this world too highly: it is a far cry from the schoolboy in his humble room in Montmartre to the Academician in his luxury apartment with white-gloved footmen. Moreover, extremely sensitive to hostile criticism, Romains was only too keen to accept praise, however extravagant. Much of the French criticism of his work has emanated from a close group of friends and admirers, and its undoubted merits have been obscured by a tendency towards eulogy. But these aspects of Romains, irritating though they may be, cannot permanently invalidate his work. Once again, we should draw the comparison with Hugo, who—on a different level—often writes with breathtaking arrogance and egoism. The reader learns to make allowances for this foible in a great writer, and to attempt a balanced view. Such a critical estimate is the aim of the present work.

Contents

Chronology

1942	Settles in Mexico City.
1944	*Bertrand de Ganges.*
1946	Elected to the Académie Française. Returns to France.
1949	*Le Moulin et l'hospice.*
1951	*Violation de frontières.*
1956	*Le Fils de Jerphanion.*
1959	*Mémoires de Madame Chauverel.*
1961	*Un grand honnête homme.*
1964	*Ai-je fait ce que j'ai voulu?*
1970	*Amitiés et rencontres.*
1972	August 14: Dies in Paris, aged 86.

CHAPTER 1

Early Years

E XAMINING Jules Romains's vast literary output, the reader may well be surprised and disappointed to find no formal memoirs. Apart from the great intrinsic interest of an immensely full and keenly-experienced life, how much light it would cast on the springs of his creative activity and thought! Yet as so often, Romains himself reflected on this question, and in the preface of his last book, *Amitiés et rencontres*, explained why he never undertook an autobiography.[1] Certainly the material was not lacking, although he never kept any regular diary; but he disliked the tendency of memoirs to become special pleading, arranged to improve the writer's image, with conscious distortion or at the least the inevitable lapses of memory. He himself, although he retained a sharp memory of individual incidents, often could not place them in relation to each other and was hazy about dates; which is why *Amitiés et rencontres* consists of a discontinuous series of memories, crystallized around separate individuals, rather than an integrated autobiography. To this explanation we may add Romains's longstanding distaste for exposure of his private life.

Nevertheless, a considerable amount of biographical material on Romains does exist. In the first place, here and there in his works he refers to events in his own life, and the book just referred to contains accounts of various literary and other friendships. Naturally, too, he drew on personal experience for many episodes in his poems, plays and novels, especially in the figure of Pierre Jallez in *Les Hommes de Bonne Volonté*; but great caution is needed in extrapolating from material written for precise artistic ends to hypothetical personal experiences lying beneath. For external evidence, André Cuisenier knew Romains from their schooldays, and this knowledge is reflected in his three critical works, while many of the facts and anecdotes in Madeleine Berry's books on Romains must evidently have been told her by the writer himself. André Bourin's *Connaissance de Jules Romains* contains, along with Bourin's text, extensive comments by Romains himself. And in the last few years Romains's first wife, writing under the name of

Gabrielle Romains, has published no less than six books dealing with her life before and after her marriage. The earlier ones are lightly fictionalized, with Romains becoming Philippe Turner and herself Geneviève Darcy; later books abandon all such pretense. Although appearing hastily written, and containing definite omissions and inaccuracies of detail, these books include extracts from Romains's letters and there is no reason to believe that her attractive picture of Romains in the years from the Lycée Condorcet to his increasing fame and success after World War I is anything but substantially true. By and large, we are in a position to follow the main lines of Romains's career.

I *Childhood*

The future writer began life as Louis-Henri-Jean Farigoule. When, still in his teens, he began to publish, he took the literary pseudonym of Jules Romains, and in 1953 legally changed his name to this. In adopting a pseudonym for literary purposes, a practice more common in France than in the Anglo-Saxon world, and sanctified by the examples of Molière, Voltaire, and Anatole France among many others, Romains was no doubt stating his firm intention of separating his private life, even his academic career, from his literary ambitions. (About the same time his closest friend, Léon Debille, also took the literary name by which he is now remembered, Georges Chennevière.) Only Romains himself could explain exactly why he chose the name he did; one theory is that he based it on the name of the Italian painter, Giulio Romano, which becomes in French Jules Romain. This seems at best unlikely, and the alternative theory is that a much greater Roman, Julius Caesar, furnished the idea for the name, which thus exemplifies both the enormous ambitions and the pride of the young author.

Romains was born in the hamlet of La Chapuze, overlooking the small town of Saint-Julien-Chapteuil in the area of the Velay. The Velay, high up towards the source of the Loire in the mountains of South-Central France, is one of the most striking and probably least-known regions in the country. Above all the visitor is impressed with the *puys*, stark volcanic cones jutting upwards from the valleys and often crowned with a chapel or church. Life is harsh in the long winters for the inhabitants, who are said to possess the hardy qualities and sturdy independence ascribed to all such mountain-dwellers. Both Romains's father, Henri Farigoule, and his mother, Marie Richier, came from longstanding Velay families, but the father, having obtained an education beyond the normal and become a schoolteacher, had left the district to teach—and live—in the Montmartre area of Paris. The accident of school holidays spent with relatives explains Romains's birth in the Velay, and within weeks the family was back in Paris. And it was there that Romains lived until he was nineteen, with most of his summer holidays spent with relatives in the Velay.

Under the influence of Taine's deterministic theories of literary creation, a good deal of effort and ingenuity, mostly misplaced, has been spent during the last century in attempting to link the essence of a writer's work not only to his heredity, but also to his geographical antecedents and even to those of his parents. André Gide is a case in point. Hints of the same line of reasoning have emerged in critical articles on Romains. The Velay has played a large part in certain of his works, notably as the background of Jerphanion in *Les Hommes de Bonne Volonté*, and in *Cromedeyre-le-Vieil*. So has Nice, in *La Douceur de la vie*. We might also note that Romains has twice acquired property in the provinces, but neither time in the Velay: a house at Hyères, on the Mediterranean, and an estate in Touraine. Paris has loomed much larger, providing not only the setting, but also the theme of much of Romains's *œuvre*. This surely points to environment rather than heredity as the key: his parents, married in 1884, were themselves recent migrants to Paris and heredity could play no part in the deep emotions raised in the young Romains by the metropolis. Certain qualities attributed to the Velay peasant might, it is true, be discerned in him: above all the ability to work hard and long, to persevere with a task once undertaken, to battle with any obstacle, in a word, the fantastic energy which has characterized Romains's career. We might be tempted to add the evidently shrewd business sense which has made him a wealthy man while bringing him an international reputation. But a mixture of intellectual ability and solid effort, put to the service of high ambition, does not necessarily imply Velay or peasant origins. The ultimate origins of artistic creativity are at present—and will no doubt continue to be—unfathomable; with this situation the critic must remain content. On a more prosaic sociological level, we should however note that

Romains forms a clear example of the development through three generations from a humble station in life to the intellectual élite, resulting from the greater social mobility and educational opportunities of the Third Republic, so clearly portrayed by Georges Duhamel in his series of *Pasquier* novels, exactly contemporaneous with *Les Hommes de Bonne Volonté*.

Romains's childhood was spent in several small apartments in Montmartre, all on the Northern, less fashionable slope. In those days Montmartre, still partly rural but rapidly being built up, if already the haunt of artists and bohemians, was not yet the tourist magnet it later became. Its inhabitants were mainly ordinary people, poor but respectable, employed in the shops and offices of central Paris, and increasingly in the factories of the Plaine Saint-Denis which were mushrooming to the North. For Montmartre looks both ways: not only over the business center of Paris down to the Seine and then to the Left Bank, but also across the smoke-obscured industrial plateau of the Northern suburbs. Both aspects were to leave profound traces in the imagination of the young Romains. Only the bare outlines of his early years are known: a brilliant and precocious child, he attended the primary school where his father taught until, at the age of ten, he was able to transfer, through the new governmental policy of free secondary education for the children of teachers, to the junior section of the famous Lycée Condorcet. There he remained for the next nine years, passing into the main school and later into the grueling *khâgne*, the post-baccalaureate preparatory course for the even more celebrated École Normale Supérieure, usually known as Normale.

II   *A Literary Vocation*

Romains's schooldays were on the surface happy and uneventful: obedient, studious, always at the top of his class, apparently following the path his parents early marked out for him. By dint of academic success, he too would become a teacher, but would go beyond the comparatively limited studies and position of *instituteur* to reach the more prestigious rank of *professeur*. An only child usually implies a lonely child, and certainly Romains seems to have had few friends until well into his teens. Nor did his father's slim salary allow for expensive hobbies or amusements, and we may imagine that he was kept studying hard, as far as possible away from undesirable frequentations. Despite his parents' protective feelings and warm affection for their son, it is possible to detect a certain reserve or lack of full intimacy; and a note written many years later by Romains indicates this. After his father's death in 1933, he was greatly astonished to discover from his mother that she was in fact Henri Farigoule's second wife, the first having died shortly after the marriage. For almost fifty years neither parent had ever told Romains of this.[2]

Two of the principal formative influences of Romains's early teens should be mentioned: his long keen-eyed walks round Paris, especially in the poorer quarters to the North and East, and his leisure reading. Without public libraries in those days, without the money to buy books for himself, he was limited to the resources of his father's painstakingly built-up collection: few titles, but all of them classics. He was thus brought up on Homer, Virgil, Lucretius, and moderns such as Goethe and Victor Hugo, the last two providing models for the literary vocation he had felt from his earliest childhood, as the finest profession open to man. And from his endless peregrinations around Paris, Romains not only acquired an unparalleled feeling for, and knowledge of, its topography which he has put to excellent literary use, but above all a mystical sense of harmony with the pulsating life of the modern metropolis which forms such an essential part of the doctrine of Unanimism.

To this must be added a severe religious crisis in his early teens. Romains was brought up as a practising Catholic, although his father was an *instituteur*, this profession being the fiercest opponents of clerical influence on the young. By fourteen he had ceased to believe, but the spiritual torments he underwent are central in his early poetry: in the 1925 preface to *La Vie Unanime*, he writes with unusual emotion of having been "a child overwhelmed by religion, made ill by religion."[3] As a result, in part at least, Unanimism would provide the psychological function of a religion-substitute. Moreover, although formal religious belief ceased at this point, a mystical streak remained in him, while several of his most impressive characters, far from unsympathetically treated, have been priests. In later life he was even to write a book, if not his most memorable, called *Interviews avec Dieu*. At the time, however, such consolation as he was able to find from the conviction that life was without apparent meaning and that Catholic doctrine was unacceptable, came above all from his reading of Lucretius.

Romains began to write early. We know of a comedy, in verse, written at nine, and a five-act political drama, *Tsar*, on the life of Boris Godunov, at fifteen. However, in his later teens, he turned to poetry, and it was with a volume of verse that he first launched into the literary world, at the age of eighteen. All in all, the picture we have of Romains in his early years is one of an adolescent of unusual intelligence and sensitivity, fired with a burning vocation for literature and with unlimited, almost arrogant ambition. In personal relationships, he seems to have been somewhat shy, perhaps another result of being an only child, and jealously watched over by his mother. (The choice of a pen name may indeed have been partly prompted by a desire to remove his literary activities from too close parental inspection and incomprehension.) In 1905, Romains passed the examination into Normale brilliantly, entering second in the section of Letters, having failed the previous year—no dishonor, in view of the extreme difficulty of this most competitive test—and gained the *Licence ès Lettres* the same year. There remained the question of army service; as a student, he was able to take advantage of the reduction in service to a single year, which he served in an infantry regiment at Pithiviers, a small town some fifty miles south of Paris. Army life came as a devastating shock to the sensitive student, paradoxically in view of his professed mystical solidarity with the Unanimist group. The reality of contact with no doubt ignorant and brutish fellow soldiers affected Romains so deeply that he was obliged to rent a room in the town, where he could at least spend occasional hours of solitude. When recalled for reserve service a few years later, Romains developed nervous stomach trouble, and was thereafter exempt from active duty. Nevertheless, army life produced ambivalent reactions in the young author: as well as disgust for its coarseness and stupidity, a certain admiration for military force and comradeship. Both were to provide literary themes.

In late 1906, Romains began his three years at Normale, taking a *licence* in science as well as the *agrégation* in philosophy. This famous institution in the Rue d'Ulm behind the Panthéon has turned out many writers and politicians as well as professors, which is its primary purpose, and Romains entered fully into life there, with its intense academic activity enlivened by elaborate practical jokes or *canulars*. Romains's own efforts in the latter field included a mock medical examination of the current intake, the nomination of a local crackpot in Paris elections, and later a hoax involving the election of a *Prince des Penseurs*, modeled on the *Prince des Poètes*, which even took in the *Figaro* newspaper. As well as the intense activity of student life, Romains was becoming increasingly known in the literary world, and with the publication of *La Vie Unanime* in 1908, his reputation was established. Already, by 1906, he had become friendly with the Abbaye group of poets (Duhamel, René Arcos, Luc Durtain, Charles Vildrac, and others), named after their unsuccessful attempt at communal living and publishing at the Abbaye de Créteil. Romains did not share in this venture, but was a sympathetic onlooker; equally, the Abbaye group did not accept the tenets of Unanimism, although they had in common the aim of writing a more direct type of poetry dealing with the everyday concerns of modern life.

Romains began his teaching career in 1909 as Professor of Philosophy at the Lycée at Brest, moving on to Laon in 1910 where he continued to teach until the War. By all accounts, he was an efficient and respected teacher, but his main energies were devoted to his literary career and he spent as much time as possible in Paris. By 1914, he had already a dozen volumes to his name and was generally regarded as one of the leading figures of the rising literary generation. The circles he moved in had brought him in contact with such figures as Moréas, Gide, Apollinaire, Max Jacob, and even Picasso. In 1912 he married Gabrielle Gaffé, the daughter of a painter friend of his father; they had known each other since 1905, but had been separated by an unhappy episode resulting in her marriage to another man and subsequent divorce. After the marriage, the couple set up house in Paris, Romains traveling to Laon several days a week to teach. Increasing prosperity brought with it the ability to travel more widely than the bicycle trips of student days, and from 1909 on Romains visited various countries in Western Europe including Italy, Germany, Switzerland, the Low Countries, and Britain. When his means permitted him to buy a car, his mobility increased, and, though scarcely a pioneer, he became acquainted with the joys and tribulations of motoring in its infancy. This all might seem to be a career of growing and uninterrupted success, and in many ways it was. Yet beneath the surface we detect a note of sadness, especially in works such as *Odes* and *Mort de quelqu'un*; and there seems little doubt that his relationship with Gabrielle during her first marriage caused him much distress. But the real shock came with the outbreak of war in 1914, which took Romains, in common with practically all his generation, almost completely by surprise. This was to prove the event which would overshadow his attitudes and literary work for the remainder of his life.

III   *The Unanimist Vision*

What we have seen of the young Romains shows us a brilliantly intelligent youth, vibrating with sensitivity, endowed with a profound sense of vocation towards literature, and determined to fulfill that vocation. But these qualities alone were not enough: intelligence, sensitivity, and sense of vocation are far from uncommon, yet much more is needed to create a durable literary career. For the would-be writer the initial major problem is what, given his sense of vocation, he shall write about. Immediately following is one of a more practical nature: having started to write, how to get himself into print. In Romains's case, the initial problem of a subject was solved by his conception of "Unanimism," and, as the conception preceded any published writings, we shall examine it at this point. A close analysis, though essential, implies certain difficulties, since Unanimism, like any other literary concept, evolved through the years, and his explanations of it at different times are not identical. The usual account of the birth of Unanimism is fairly clear:[4] one evening in October, 1903, when Romains and Chennevière were walking up the crowded Rue d'Amsterdam, Romains had the sudden vision that the whole city, shops, passersby, cabs, formed a vast unity, with its own collective consciousness, to which he himself had intuitive access. Now perhaps the critic should view with some caution such sudden experiences in writers' formative years: they form dramatic episodes in biographical legends, but may, as in the case of Flaubert's "epileptic" attack or Valéry's "nuit de Gênes," inexplicable in themselves, tell us little about the sources of creative imagination. Or again they may merely act as a crystallization of tendencies and attitudes already present: we may instance Claudel's "conversion" in Notre-Dame Cathedral, and almost certainly Romains's experience in the Rue d'Amsterdam. Even without this, there is no reason why the concept of Unanimism should not have developed in precisely the same way.

At the same time, the episode as described points to certain key elements in the concept of Unanimism. First and foremost, it is an intuitive concept rather than the product of rational analysis, whatever part intelligence may have played in its elaboration once the primary intuition had taken place. Secondly, this intuition of the collectivity: the city, the crowded urban group, is positive and optimistic, and incidentally at the other pole from the typical Romantic love of Nature and solitude. Finally, the collectivity does not exist passively by itself: it requires the active consciousness of the observer, Romains himself, at a definite moment in time. It follows from this that Romains is somehow privileged in possessing this intuitive access to the group consciousness, and that the point in time where he can exercise it is itself a "privileged moment."

Given the basic concept, Romains's problem was solved: he would translate the intuition into literary works—poetry and prose seem to have tempted him equally from the start. And the concept would be given a name: after careful consideration of various possibilities, he and Chennevière arrived at the term of *Unanimisme*, which they promptly set about publicizing in articles and critical essays.[5] This desire to create a literary movement was of course in no way unusual; indeed, we may suspect that many would-be poets found it easier to compose manifestos than write poetry. Some sixty literary *-isms* in France about 1905 have been listed ranging from *Paroxysme* through *Somptuarisme* to *Métabolisme;*[6] many of these were doubtless frivolous, and only two are still heard of today, Marinetti's Futurism and Unanimism. Romains rapidly showed himself perfectly aware of the publicity potential of Unanimism, and made full use of it. We should not, however, blame a young author for doing what he can within broad bounds to attract attention to his work; and in the decade ending in 1914, we find a good deal of logrolling among Romains, Chennevière and the Abbaye poets, writing glowing reviews of each other's books and espousing each other's quarrels. Once successfully launched, they tended to go their separate ways.

Nor should we suspect Romains of insincerity in the initial conception of Unanimism. All the evidence is that it grew directly out of Romains's religious crisis in his teens, and in essence provided a defense against metaphysical solitude, even a substitute religion. This is borne out by a famous couplet from *La Vie Unanime*:

. . . pour nous consoler de la vie éternelle
Nous aurons la vie unanime[7]

no less than by the very terminology. Unanimism implies that the group has a single soul, the *unanime*, and once created, it becomes, explicitly, a *dieu*. Viewed as a substitute religion, Unanimism is unimpressive; it has a natural appeal to the gregariousness of youth, but the solidarity of the group is no defense against individual death. It is even weaker than the post-Romantic religion of art, which at least offers the artist survival through his works (and Romains, if unconsciously, shared this religion too in his belief in the vocation of the artist). Unanimism is not so much a philosophy as an attitude of mind, a *Weltanschauung*, which no doubt furnished solace to Romains and Chennevière, but was immensely useful as a literary doctrine, not so much expressing fundamental verities as providing the two with a springboard for their creative imagination. This point should be elaborated as the issue has been confused by Romains himself. Writing a preface in 1957 to a somewhat eccentric philosophical work by Noël Martin-Deslias, he praises the latter for having "given to Unanimism its true place in the development of human thought." Unanimism, he claims, was neither a means of publicity-seeking nor a minute episode of literary history, but "one of the principal phases of human evolution": indeed, the *cogitamus* should be compared to Descartes's *cogito*.[8] We must take this with a pinch of salt. In 1925, in his clearest outline of Unanimist ideas, Romains stated categorically that Unanimism could not be assimilated to a philosophical system, since it had neither its structure nor its logical coherence, but was primarily a mental attitude, which he did, however, expect to become almost universally adopted as time went on. It implied two acts of faith: belief in a spiritual reality, a concept in fact absent from initial Unanimist theory, but later named the "psychic continuum"; and secondly, acceptance of the idea that we can enter into direct intuitive communion with this psychic continuum. This analysis makes much more sense than his later claims—quite apart from any considerations of modesty. The psychic continuum is itself a vague concept, deriving no doubt ultimately from the pantheistic Evolutionism of Hugo, and so broad as to be incapable of exact definition. It can even be compared with Jung's Collective Unconscious; or again used as justification for Romains's later interest in phenomena such as hypnotism, clairvoyance, and telepathy.

We may also see it as a justification for his belief that the great artist, such as Balzac, has intuitive powers of psychological understanding unknown to the layman. Romains's own practice, in his novels, of characterization, often consists of "looking into the minds" of his characters by such means as interior monologue and reported thought.

Nor was the concept anywhere near as original as Romains thought and claimed. Both Lamartine and Michelet used the very word *unanime*, in a similar sense, while Baudelaire describes the *jouissances fiévreuses* of communion with the crowd in his prose poem *Les Foules*. Other literary ancestors must include Zola, who frequently shows the domination of the individual by the group, notably in the crowd scenes at the riot in *Germinal* or the sale in *Au Bonheur des Dames*, though we should note that Romains's optimism stems more probably from Hugo. Zola's crowds tend to be destructive, and he has little faith in their rationality. Verhaeren, too, offers an even closer parallel, in his belief in the poet's communion with his surroundings; but Romains has denied any influence from Walt Whitman's *Leaves of Grass*, which he did not read until later.[9] Attempts have also been made to link Unanimism with French sociological thought, and here again Romains has reacted with vigorous denials. The power of the collective had been extensively treated by Gustave Le Bon in *Psychologie des Foules* (1895), and Gabriel Tarde in *L'Opinion et la Foule* (1901). These works had been widely diffused—and for that matter are still well worth reading—but it is wrong to try to link Romains's Unanimism with them, since both authors are basically hostile to crowds, which they see as several degrees of civilization lower than the individual, potential mobs too easily swayed by a *meneur*.

With Émile Durkheim, the problem is more complex. Since he was Professor of Pedagogy at the Sorbonne from 1902, Romains could scarcely have escaped knowing something about his work when he became a student at Normale. Yet we may take in good faith Romains's assurance that he had not read a word of Durkheim until after the completion of *La Vie Unanime* in 1907. In any case, despite the parallelism of certain ideas, Romains's conception is a good deal cruder than the subtle analyses of one of the greatest of sociologists. There is, too, a fundamental difference in emphasis: in drawing attention to the hidden springs of social behavior, Durkheim shows that the idea of man as individual is historically posterior to the idea of him as a member of a social group. However, this is not to claim that the development of individualism is a degeneration, and, with Romains, to place the group as the higher stage.

A similar parallel can be noted with the work of Bergson, with which Romains must obviously have become familiar as a philosophy student. Here too the initial conception of Unanimism perhaps antedated close familiarity with Bergson's ideas, but the stress on a virtually mystical intuition rather than rational comprehension, as the basis of knowledge, is clearly common to both. Bergson's *perception immédiate* is reflected in Romains's idea of *poésie immédiate*, poetry as the result of spontaneous apprehension of reality, perceived in Unanimist groups. This perception is, moreover, seen in terms of joy, and another parallel may be drawn here with Gide's *Nourritures terrestres*; implied is the idea of the transmutation of prosaic everyday life into a superior level of existence by means of "privileged moments." For Romains makes a clear distinction between *vivre* and *exister*, *vivre* being dull meaningless life unilluminated by Unanimism, which alone can raise it to the superior level of *exister*. It is noteworthy that this distinction bears a striking similarity to Sartre's concept of *être-en-soi* and *être-pour-soi*, but in any case behind both—and behind the idea of the privileged moment—lies the Romantic view of intensity as the criterion of living. This apparent optimism is further reflected on the political plane. Romains's sympathies in the years before 1914 were generally with the Left, with the Socialism of Jaurès, one of whose speeches he had heard as a child. But he had not worked out his position in any detail, and the true degree of his political sophistication, about 1904, is indicated by the fact that in choosing a name for his group conception, he seriously considered that of "Communism" before arriving at Unanimism. Again, its latent authoritarian trends would make him admire Briand's energy in suppressing the 1910 general strike. Attempts were even made by critics belonging to the extreme Right-wing *Action Française* group to "assimilate" Romains's Unanimism, though his *dieux* did not include the Nation, stopping at the City. His attitude towards war was equally ambivalent. On the one hand, universal communion of mankind ought to be the highest manifestation of the Unanimist urge, and he seems to have shared the belief of Jaurès (and Durkheim) that industrial development would strengthen social solidarity, rendering war impossible. On the other hand, he was keenly attracted by the sheer power of an army, exerted necessarily against other groups. This inconsistency was never to be resolved within the framework of Unanimism, although Romains came to see, after the First War, and even more after the development of repressive dictatorship in Italy and Germany, the destructive possibilities inherent in enthusiasm for the group. The parallel with Marinetti is instructive: starting with a somewhat similar glorification of the modern world of technology, he brought out his Futurist Manifesto in 1909, only to turn a virulent Fascist, reveling in sheer irrational force, in the 1920's. By then Romains had toned down his earlier views considerably. The Unanimism of the barracks, painfully learnt in 1905, was only a short march from the Unanimism of the concentration camp. The crucial element lacking in early Unanimism was indeed the controlling power of reason, without which lasting human progress is impossible; yet reason is an individual faculty, whereas the group as such, incapable of rational thought, simply indulges in collective emotions.

We may also doubt whether Unanimism was in fact as optimistic as it on the surface appeared. As a substitute religion, it is a reaction to Romains's metaphysical anguish at a world bereft of God, and a note of pessimism is evident in certain of Romains's writings from the start, running parallel with the high spirits of books like *Les Copains*. So joy is inseparable from anguish as the two poles of Romains's creative imagination: a recent German critic has indeed treated Romains's entire literary career in terms of affirmation of life, and flight from life.[10]

What Romains is really doing is not intuitively communing with the "soul" of a collectivity, but applying his keen sensitivity and imagination to the world around him. In practice, the whole notion of the group soul is no more than a metaphor, and once seen as such the religious connotations melt away. The collective emotions undoubtedly felt, and differences in human behavior brought about, by membership in a group are phenomena reducible to psychological, not to religious terms. Moreover, that Unanimism is primarily a literary doctrine is proved by the need for its experience to find imaginative expression. Thus the writer remains dominant: the suprahuman reality with which he claims to be in communion is instead ordered through his individual creative imagination. Frequently, indeed, it is as an outsider that Romains perceives the

Unanimist reality he treats: on a journey, or a walk through a quarter of Paris not his own. We must note, too, a certain contradiction between the idea of poetry as a kind of spontaneous outpouring, and the highly conscious and willed nature of much of Romains's verse, both in structure and in versification. This necessary superiority over his material naturally leads to a kind of authoritarian position, reinforced by the belief that it is his superior powers of intuition which are responsible. So, despite the notion of the individual communing with the group, supposedly the higher reality, we inevitably are really faced with the group subservient to the artist, that is, Romains himself. This is the basic difficulty in Unanimism, and probably the reason why, although much discussed, it gained few adherents. Romains warmly denied that Unanimism was in any way a literary school, with a leader and disciples,[11] but the movement was everywhere coupled with his name. Duhamel, who as a close friend was on the receiving end of Romains's eloquence in the early years, could not forbear from pointing out, when receiving Romains into the Académie Française forty years later, that "if Unanimism did not become a religion, with its dogma, its clergy, its temples, its heresies and its sects," it was not Romains's fault.[12]

Ultimately we must see Unanimism as Romains's poetic vision of the world, gradually changing in emphasis, and becoming less dogmatic until, by about 1925, it appears simply one of various aspects of his mature outlook. As such, it follows the example of all -isms, for no lasting literary work has ever been totally explicable in terms of a movement, with no reference to the individual creative imagination of its author. Chennevière's attitude to Unanimism shows differences, apart from his work being much narrower in scope.[13] Romains's vision is indeed highly personal, composed as it is of his knowledge of Paris, particularly Montmartre and the Northern industrial areas, and of the Velay. This surprising, almost inconsistent mixture of a little-known rural landscape with the bustling capital seen specifically in terms of modern industry and technology, forms the setting of most of his early writings, yet is not logically tied to Unanimist theory, being simply the accident of his upbringing. Stripped of its externals, it proves highly individualistic. The conception would be outgrown, but it provided him with the inspiration for two decades of vigorous literary activity.

CHAPTER 2

Apprenticeship

I *Earliest Works*

R OMAINS's first book of poems was written while he was still
a schoolboy at the age of seventeen and eighteen. This extreme
literary precocity, while not to be compared with that of Rimbaud,
should nevertheless not be forgotten especially as this earliest
poetry, in part derivative as is only to be expected, rises occasionally
to heights of mature technique. Not all of the early poems have
survived: Romains submitted a manuscript to the *Société des
Poètes Français*, of which about one-third were selected and published by them in 1904 under the title of *L'Âme des Hommes*, and
the remainder lost. The thirty pages which appeared are divided
into four sections: *La Ville consciente, Les Hommes, Les Âmes*, and
L'Âme du Poète; of these, *La Ville consciente* was printed in its
entirety, and the three other sections truncated. The collection shows
clearly the poetic inheritance of Unanimism: the Baudelaire of
Tableaux parisiens, and the Hugo of a swelling faith in the future of
humanity. There might at first sight seem a contradiction between
the two, but this dissolves when we see that Romains, using Baudelaire's interest in curious aspects of modern Paris, replaces his
pessimism by Hugo's confident hopes. Thus, in *La Ville*:

> *Les Désirs attroupés comme des taureaux noirs*
> *Entrechoquent leurs fronts dans la nuit et mugissent;*
> *Le sol est une source immense d'où jaillissent*
> *Flots de joie et vapeurs d'espoirs.*[1]

The first line here might be a pastiche of Baudelaire, but the optimistic note is that of Hugo. Other verses echo Hugo's style as well as his
vision:

> *Je suis réellement, je suis immensément;*
>
> .   .   .   .
> *Je suis la vision vague de la clarté.*
>
> .   .   .   .
> *C'est pour moi que la glèbe accouche et qu'elle souffre,*

> *Tous ses enfantements convergent vers mon gouffre*
> *Mais je les engloutis pour les magnifier,*
> *Car je suis le robuste et géant ouvrier.*[2]

It is in the nature of novice poets to be less original than they think, and the seasoned reader will also detect echoes of other poets, such as Verlaine, Laforgue, or Verhaeren. The Baudelaire of *L'Invitation au Voyage* is also evident, while an entire poem, *L'Âme du Soir*, draws its inspiration from *Crépuscule du Soir*. Perhaps the best poems in the collection are contained in the final section. *Ode à la machine* is a slightly self-conscious but striking acknowledgment of the place of machinery in the modern world; we may contrast it with *Avant*, where Romains, using similar elements from industrial life, achieves the personal note of his later poetry:

> . . . . *Il me semble*
> *Que je suis sur un quai désert dans une gare.*
>
> *L'immense hall vitré que le soleil bigarre*
> *Abrite des rumeurs qui vont s'enfuir du nid;*
> *Le choc de deux wagons vides qu'on réunit*
> *Applique un soufflet sec et froid sur les murailles,*
> *Puis retentit plus sourd au fond de mes entrailles.*
>
> . . . .
> *Mon âme est trouble comme un matin de bataille.*[3]

We should note that although Romains has developed certain Unanimist themes, such as the vision of the modern city as a living, positive entity into which the poet's individuality may be merged, in form these poems are entirely traditional, with strict rhyme and meter. Not even the most pedantic critic could fault him; to this extent at least, the adolescent Romains was perfectly prepared to conform.

We should not make too much of this earliest collection, particularly since it has never been reprinted (Romains lost his own copy during World War II) and exists only in a handful of learned libraries. Romains's themes are already sketched out, while technical ability, despite imitation, is undeniable. His success in having a work published so young was able to give him an additional burst of confidence, both in the rightness of his chosen vocation, and in executing the individual projects germinating in his imagination.

A very different work is the *Poème du Métropolitain*, written in

October, 1904, and published in June, 1905, in the *Revue Littéraire de Paris et de Champagne*; it was not to appear in volume form until it came out as one of *Deux Poèmes* in 1910, with a prefatory note explaining its background. The *Poème du Métropolitain* takes as its subject a journey on the Paris subway, at the time still a recent innovation. In form it is an extended prose poem, except for two short sections in *vers libres*. In fact, however, the work could equally well be regarded as lyrical prose, such is the hybrid nature of the prose poem. The subway is treated as a *unanime*, by which the individual is gripped; Romains's technique is largely to "personify" or rather to turn the subway into a living, savage animal:

> *Les mâchoires de la station s'ouvrent et crèvent le trottoir, comme un crocodile qui somnole à fleur d'eau, et dont le bâillement déchire le fleuve.*[4]

Again, the train with its load of passengers becomes *un seul être vertigineux ayant conscience d'aller.*[5] The parallel with the mine in Zola's *Germinal* or the express in *La Bête humaine* may be unconscious; it is nonetheless evident. Even the air is made alive and turned into a monstrous being which swallows up the passengers in its maw: everyone who has traveled on the Paris Métro has recognized its unmistakable aroma. In this way is produced the birth of a *dieu*, and the religious imagery is explicit:

> *Dans cette crèche, plus morne et plus nue que la crèche de Bethléem, les hommes lassés des vérités caduques peuvent venir contempler la naissance d'un dieu.*[6]

Romains goes on to celebrate the savage elemental joy of rapid movement, as the train hurls itself through the tunnels; his language reaches heights of extravagant lyricism as he describes this intuition of a reality more exciting than any dream:

> *Les cauchemars les plus rares de l'âme qui s'isole ne valent pas la réalité que je cherche et que je palpe à travers l'ombre.*[7]

Despite derivative elements and an exaggerated sense of exaltation, the *Poème du Métropolitain* is specifically "modern" poetry, transforming into a collective adventure what was, if fairly new, nevertheless an ordinary experience of Parisian life in the age of machinery and technological invention. From a consideration of this poem and *L'Âme des Hommes*, two facts emerge. First, Romains was in full possession of most of the central ideas of Unanimism. Further elaboration of the doctrine would be made, but its essentials are clear. Secondly, he had not yet fully developed his verse technique, and was still casting about to find an adequate vehicle. In *L'Âme des Hommes*, his prosody is entirely traditional; here Rimbaud and Verhaeren appear to be the models, both of the form itself and of its exalted tone. It is only after this point in his career, that is, not until about 1905, that Romains first evolved the poetic techniques which have since been associated with his name.

II   *The New Versification*

Before treating his first major poetical work, *La Vie Unanime*, we should therefore examine these techniques, which are explicitly listed in the *Petit traité de versification*, published jointly with Chennevière in 1923, and based on lectures given at the École du Vieux-Colombier in 1921–1922. (Though this was a joint publication, we may surmise that Romains played a dominating part.) The aim is extremely ambitious: not only to illustrate the two poets' own idea of prosody, as had recently been done by Duhamel and Vildrac in *Notes sur la technique poétique* (1910), but also to lay their precepts down in a formal treatise which would effectively replace the traditional rules of Malherbe. This normative intention is quite explicit, and the book is a curious mixture of exposition of conventional prosody, lucid analysis of the formal development of French poetry in the nineteenth century, and affirmation of Romains's and Chennevière's own practice as being the way—the only way— to enrich French poetry in the future.

The authors see the need to broaden poetic techniques, but reject the idea of *vers libres*, which they see as in effect indistinguishable from prose except by subjective decision and arbitrary typographical form. Nor do they accept devices such as the suppression of the mute "e" in counting syllables, although they have no objection to rhyming singular with plural, or in general the poet's own choice of diphthongs as either single or double syllables. For them, poetic diction should not be confused with colloquial speech, and the poet should therefore avoid the contractions and deformations of the latter. The main originality of the theories advanced, however, lies in the addition of *accords* to the traditional resources of rhyme, *accords* being defined as *un rapport de sonorités de sons entre voyelles*

. . . et pour élément auxiliaire un rappel de consonnes.[8] Examples given are *buste/peste, ruche/rêche*; and in fact these *accords* are further subdivided into masculine, feminine, mixed, adequate, and rich, in the same way as traditional rhyme. Moreover, rhyme itself is broadened to include such additional nonconventional categories as *rime imparfaite* (multi*tudes*/amer*tume*; E*urope*/*roc*; and even *jaunes/autre*); *rime par augmentation* (amor*ti*/domes*tique*); *rime par diminution* (*étoiles/toits*); *rime renversée*, the reversal of two consonants around the final vowel (ju*lep*/archi*pel*; ma*chine*/pé*niche*); and even further refinements such as *rime renversée imparfaite* (cor*tège*/pro*phète*).[9] Rhymes need no longer conclude individual verses, since a new concept of *rime avancée* is proposed:

> *J'ai des o*reilles *qui me brûlent,*
>
> . . . .
>
> *Ne me parle plus de M*ar*seille.*

At this point, not least because of the droll qualities of some of the examples given, we begin to wonder if an element of mystification is not also present. We read, for instance, with astonishment, that:

> *On pense être la* chair *d'un cou, plein de sang âcre,*
> *Un cou trop court que l'étoffe* rêche *irrite* . . .

is a *rime renversée mixte avancée de 6* [*pieds*] *au premier et de 2 au second* [*vers*]—or that

> *Un mous*tique *est pris d'appé*tit . . .

constitutes an example of *rime intérieure par diminution.*[10] A similar schema is devised of *accords par augmentation* (s'égaie/ transfi*gurent*), *accords par diminution, accords renversés* (masculine: *cor*/va*rech*; feminine: *riche/chère*; mixed: *tour/rate*); *accords renversés imparfaits.* Here the authors admit that a single consonant would produce a virtually imperceptible effect (sa*c*/*c*ol); a group of two consonants would be necessary (au*tre*/*tr*oupe). Again, these *accords* could be advanced, and indeed neither of them need take a terminal position. Thus

> *Le pé*ril *tourne alentour;*
> *un pas* écrase *les feuilles.* . . .

is an "accord *imparfait mixte avancé* de 4 au premier et de 3 au second."[11] The authors' attitude to meter is similarly more inclusive

than in traditional prosody, yet they remain firm in their belief
that it should be clear and systematic. In practice, Romains has at
various times used lines of from four to fourteen syllables, and the
latter with considerable skill.

These, then, are the lines on which the authors see the future of
French poetry, above all in obtaining a musical continuity inacces-
sible to classical poetic technique, by linking the different verses of
the poem with a harmonic progression of *accords*. It is difficult to
deny the effectiveness of an example like:

> *De la halte encaissée un chemin part sans* ombre;
> *Il rampe sur la plaine, puis monte et se* cambre.
> *Le clair groupe, un instant, trouve que c'est lu*gubre,
> *Ce chemin qui s'en va jaune comme un oc*tobre.
> *Mais la lumière envoie une force aux ver*tèbres.
> *Il sourit au chemin sans âme où l'on est* libre.[12]

Similarly, a sonoric progression may be seen in this series of *rimes
par diminution*: ba*raque/rat/mère/*ai*mais/plume/plu/souple/*des*sous*.

Here, perhaps, we should sit back and reflect. The principles
enunciated certainly explain the authors' own poetic practice—
and they wryly comment that even favorable critics had not been
aware of the devices used, simply supposing that these *vers accordés*
were *vers blancs*. Some of these devices had in fact been used by
earlier poets: Rimbaud's rhyming of senti*nelle* with *nulle* is quoted,
although Laforgue's practice in *Derniers vers*, at least equally
relevant, is rather surprisingly ignored. Again, assonance rather
than rhyme was the principle of medieval French poetry, and to this
extent, the *accords* have an unimpeachable ancestry. But the main
problem with the *accord* must be its tenuous nature, as the examples the authors quote of such *accords imparfaits* as *suc/sort*;
fraîche/frappe; or *roc/route*, which amount to little more than conventional alliteration. Certainly the authors were to some extent
aware of this; but one is forced to wonder if most French poets
could not be shown to have used a considerable number of *accords*
in much the same way, together of course with conventional rhyme.
Be that as it may, their position is quite clearly one of a new kind of
Classicism, and the subsequent concentration of attention on
formal considerations may very well have something to do with the
highly self-conscious nature of much of Romains's verse.

III *Fiction*

Romains's first piece of fiction came out in the review *Le Penseur* in June, 1905. Entitled *Le Rassemblement*, with the subtitle "Récit de la vie unanime," to publicize Unanimism, this four-page story has not been reprinted and has attracted little critical attention. Quite simply it describes the birth, growth, decline, and death of a Parisian group. One fine April evening a street quarrel begins between a man selling nutcrackers and another distributing prospectuses. About to come to blows, they are separated by a policeman and a crowd collects, first gradually, then more rapidly, before it moves off towards the police station, losing some of its members but gaining others, until in a street empty of traffic it develops into a firm unity again, having achieved Unanimist consciousness. At the commissariat, some of the group enter, while the rest mill about outside, soon joined by others. But the collective consciousness has disintegrated and many of the newcomers are unable even to find out the reason for the crowd. With the boredom of waiting, the group starts to shrink until the last person leaves as the gas lamps are lit; but the *rassemblement* is already dead.

Not too much need be made of this very brief tale. As an illustration of the theory of Unanimism, it is clear and convincing: a group, seen, say, from above—and Romains adopts a kind of bird's-eye perspective—might well form, move about, and disperse in precisely the way described. But this originality of conception at the same time forces certain limitations: above all, human interest is lacking—and it is the communication of human interest which provides the cement of the group itself. The quarrel which triggers off the action, though doubtless trivial, is completely unexplained, as is its outcome. This is what Romains intends, but the novel narrative viewpoint is only gained at the expense of traditional values. Indeed, it might be claimed that Romains has developed a technique, valid on occasion for special emphasis, and is using it as an infallible method. Later in his career he is willing to combine his own technique with those of the general tradition of the novel, and produces far richer results. Nevertheless the story is neatly told, in careful descriptive prose with occasional striking images, and may be taken as a vivid illustration of Unanimist theory.

Romains's second book, in 1906, was another short prose work, *Le Bourg régénéré*. Originally it bore the subtitle, "Conte de la vie

unanime"; while in the now most accessible edition, by the *N.R.F.*
in 1920, this has been changed to the more simple "Petite légende."
In fact the story may as well be called a *nouvelle*. The plot is simple.
A young man, a postal employee, arrives in a small town, and
gradually constructs his life there round his work and the daily
trivialities of existence. At this point he is being "assimilated" by
the town, which has evolved over the decades a web of collective
habits and relationships: he eats and sleeps earlier, his sexual
desires become less refined, and *ignorance* takes the place of
inquiétude. But the life of the town, if Unanimistic, is passive, and the
main action only begins when the young man, after lunching well
one Saturday, visits a public urinal and remembers how his friends
in Paris used, after a political meeting, to scribble subversive inscrip-
tions in such places. He immediately writes on the wall a sentence
which comes to mind: "The man who possesses lives at the expense
of the man who works; whoever does not produce the equivalent of
what he consumes is a social parasite."[13]

Writing this is no more than an idle joke, a *canular* in the Normale
tradition; but, sauntering round the town on this afternoon of
leisure, the young man is struck by the truth of his own slogan:
the whole town is unproductive, parasitical, and above all mediocre,
stagnating uselessly round its church, shops, cafés, brothel, weekly
market, and meetings of the municipal council. What the place
wants is "regenerating"; and ironically the scribble in the urinal is
all that is needed. In the next few days, various men read the slogan
and take it up in various ways: retired men and *rentiers* decide to
look for some worthwhile occupation, political arguments start up
in cafés, household quarrels develop. Even a priest in need of a text
is deeply influenced by the slogan: nothing similar appears in the
collections of sermons he knows. A landowner insults three pastry-
cooks and is beaten up for his pains; a wealthy young man takes the
opportunity of breaking with his mistress, a "parasite"; the beadle
sees in the slogan an appeal to procreation and turns his steps
towards the brothel, to find that prices have been reduced for
productive workers and compensatingly increased for the rich and
idle. A month later, ardor for revolution, or at least reform, has
increased steadily, while the mayor has initiated an agricultural
fair, and a clay factory and sawmill have been founded. Passive
Unanimism has been transformed into an active state, and the story
ends a year later with the town in full expansion and industrial

development. People eat later, sleep less, even read newspapers and books: the town is regenerated.

On the surface, what we have here is a Unanimist demonstration in terms of the comic: the humorous element of the story offers its main attraction today. Yet if we examine *Le Bourg régénéré* closely, we find clear evidence of other implications of Unanimism. Above all is the distinction between positive, active existence and the negative, passive life of the town before its regeneration: positive existence being identified with political reform and active industry. Moreover, the transformation requires an animator, the outsider bringing in the dynamic idea which triggers off the action. Although he does this unconsciously, it is a short step to conscious manipulation of the group by the animator, who by implication must be a superior individual able to dominate the collectivity, if indirectly. We shall find a similar animator in practically all of Romains's Unanimist works, developing finally into barefaced charlatans, while the plot of *Knock* is essentially a repeat of that of *Le Bourg régénéré*. Romains views his animator favorably, and will continue to have a weakness for his rogues; but in reality the implications of the story are not too different from Le Bon's picture of the dangerous activities of the *meneurs*. Violence is always latent in such a situation, although it is largely obscured as in *Les Copains* by the comic treatment; occasionally it becomes overt, as when an angry husband returns home and, during a marital quarrel, hurls the sleek family cat, another "parasite," out of an upper story window. Equally, any kind of vigorous political activity is seen as automatically positive, without waiting to consider its results. On another plane, the idea of knowledge through intuition is apparent: Romains states that sometimes a town may only need an hour to *s'exprimer à un passant*,[14] though an inhabitant might not obtain this knowledge in twenty years. This implies that the outsider is a superior individual with abnormal powers. (A similar notion can indeed be found in Sartre, whose debt to Bergson has not yet been satisfactorily made clear.)

Le Bourg régénéré illustrates clearly the stage reached in Romains's literary development. He can write with verve a fairly extended piece of fiction, drawing on his powers of fantasy and imagination for the plot, although the town itself is an amalgam of Pithiviers and Saint-Julien-Chapteuil; but his characters, even the animator, are insubstantial, which would show as a serious flaw in a longer work.

On its level, nevertheless, *Le Bourg régénéré* marks the successful application of Unanimism to comic purposes, a vein which was to yield Romains some of his greatest triumphs.

IV La Vie Unanime

Romains's first important and indeed best-known collection of verse is *La Vie Unanime*, published in 1908 by the Abbaye group. In it, we find a systematic exploitation of all the main themes of Unanimism; Romains had worked on it from early 1904 to August, 1907, and the volume thus spans his experiences from school through army service to life at Normale. The volume is substantial, fifty-eight poems of some 250 pages, with a clearly defined structure. There are two main sections, *Les Unanimes* and *L'Individu*, each subdivided into three: *Avant, Dieu le long des maisons*, and *Dynamisme*, followed by *Sans moi, Moi en révolte*, and *Nous*. The general line of development is the poet's gradual apprehension of Unanimist groups, then the unsuccessful struggles of the self against this intuition, until finally, full mystical communion is attained with Unanimist life. Furthermore, each poem takes a line or phrase of an earlier poem as epigraph, which binds the collection together in still closer unity. Romains has described his method of composition in an important preface to the 1925 edition: the poems were written individually, inspired by a circumstance, an emotion, a mystery suddenly revealed to him, the total aim being *un lyrisme objectif d'essence spirituelle*.[15] Since the general plan was clear in his mind, each poem would then be fitted in where seemed most appropriate. The final order is therefore not chronological, as is proved by the fact that early poems, regular in form, are found throughout alongside others using Romains's later system of *accords*. Most deal with city life, and with such familiar Unanimist groups as the theater, the church, the café, or the barracks, though a smaller number, inspired by the Velay, treat rustic life. Certain poems are largely theoretical or abstract, and these sound rather heavy and prosaic today, though they play their part in compelling the reader to apprehend the Unanimist vision. More appealing, individually, are those where Romains develops a simple idea, such as pleasure at opening a letter or disappointment at not receiving one, and where vivid imagery is not obscured by Unanimist rhetoric. Here, we should examine the idea of "poésie immédiate." Romains's aim is to convert his intuition of reality into immediate expression, without intervention of reasoning or of symbols, in this way rendering his poetry much more direct and spontaneous. It is thus largely in the present tense, and eschews suggestion for statement. His subject matter is primarily his own experiences, with recurring symbols of modern technology, such as bridges, barges, cranes, or train whistles. This note is not entirely original since "technological" poetry goes back at least as far as Maxime Du Camp's *Chants modernes* (1861), while telegraph posts and another favorite image of Romains, the tinkling of a piano heard in the street, recall Laforgue. However, *Le Moteur vit* must be one of the first poems in any language on the motorcar. Other images will provide the themes of later work: the boy with the hoop in *Les Hommes de Bonne Volonté*, the funeral procession in *Mort de quelqu'un*, or the theater in *Ode à la Foule qui est ici*. Besides recurring Unanimist images, Romains makes constant use of the deliberately startling metaphor:

> *Une fumée*
> *Frétille au dos*
> *D'une maison;*
> *Comme la queue*
> *Du chien qui trouve*
> *Un paquet d'os*
> *Sous le gazon.* [16]

> *La ville me caresse avec un bruit de fiacre.* [17]

Often too, this is linked to the Unanimist vision:

> *Je voudrais boire un bol de tumulte bouillant.* [18]

At other times, a simple lyricism predominates:

> *Il vaut mieux dormir sous les feuilles*
> *Que de savoir le sens du monde* . . . [19]

Perhaps, too, we may find the ecstatic note, particularly in the later poems, a little forced and prefer the underlying poignant melancholy:

> *Il neige depuis des années;*
> *Le ciel est si bas, si crasseux*
> *Que les hommes de haute taille*
> *Ont presque peur de s'y cogner*
> *Et d'en faire tomber sur eux.* [20]

Some poems had appeared separately before 1908, but publication of the whole collection brought Romains wide recognition. Whether or not one accepts Unanimist theory, one cannot deny the power and originality, both in form and in content, of *La Vie Unanime*. Its only comparable predecessor was Verhaeren's *Villes tentaculaires*, but Romains's directness is more forceful than Verhaeren's impressionism, and the distinction is reinforced by his stress on strict meter as against the Belgian poet's *vers libres*. Romains published *La Vie Unanime* when he was 22, and its poems go back four more years. Many respectable poets would be content to make such a volume the culmination of their achievement, but for Romains this was simply a further stage in his literary evolution.

Romains's next poem marks another new departure, since it was designed as a demonstration of Unanimism in action, specifically the inspiring of a group soul in the crowd at a theater. The poem, *À la Foule qui est ici*, was delivered on June 2, 1909, by an actor, de Max, at the Théâtre de l'Odéon, and appeared, in its entirety, in *Vers et Prose* of April-June. It was reprinted separately the same year, came out again with *Le Poème du Métropolitain* as *Deux Poèmes* in 1910, yet once more as the final poem in *Odes et Prières* in 1913, the last two times under the slightly different title of *Ode à la Foule qui est ici*.

The poem, some seventy-five lines in length, is a striking illustration of Unanimist theory in action, as well as literary creation. It begins with an affirmation of collective existence, not individual reflection, as the highest value:

> *Dix mois de spéculations abstraites*
> *Dans la solitude et le silence*
> *Ne valent pas un quart d'heure d'ici.*
>
> . . . .
>
> *Les vérités de maintenant*
> *Naissent où il y a beaucoup d'hommes,*
> *Et s'exhalent des multitudes.*[21]

The poet then addresses the crowd waiting passively. The technique is once again that of the animator; there is no question of spontaneous generation of the collective spirit:

> . . .   *tu seras, Ô Foule!*
> *Pleine de ton silence unique et de ma voix.*[22]

As he describes this process, it is presumably expected to be actually taking place, until the audience is entirely dominated by the poet, a situation reinforced by explicit use of the image of rape:

> *Ne te défends pas, foule femelle,*
> *C'est moi qui te veux, moi qui t'aurai!*[23]

Through this violence, a collective *dieu* is created, even though it will die as soon as the crowd leaves the theater:

> *Tu es mienne avant que tu sois morte;*
> *Les corps qui sont ici, la ville peut les prendre:*
> *Ils garderont au front comme une croix de cendre*
> *Le vestige du dieu que tu es maintenant.*[24]

We should perhaps treat this poem as Romains's earliest dramatic work, and, without seeing its effect on a real theater audience, it is difficult to comment on its dramatic qualities. Read as a poem, we cannot deny its ingeniosity, but equally there is present an element of contrived artificiality. Taken as a formulation of Unanimist theory, the poem furnishes a succinct expression of the domination of the passive group by the stronger-willed animator, and of the underlying violence inherent in this process.

V *Les Dieux*

In Romains's next collection, *Premier livre de Prières*, we again detect the need for a framework to link the individual poems into a united whole. Nevertheless, several of these poems, written in 1908, were printed separately in reviews before the entire book appeared in 1909. As the title indicates, Romains has a specifically religious intention: the poems are in effect invocations of a series of Unanimist *dieux, au Couple, à la Famille, à un Groupe, à la Maison, à une Rue, à un Village, à plusieurs dieux*, and finally *au plus grand dieu*, the City. This plan is in fact a highly complex poetical conceit, which may well strike us as artificial, since Romains, who evidently wished to preserve as many as possible of the mystic connotations of the idea of God or gods, does not in fact succeed in doing so, given the ordinariness of the Unanimist deities invoked. The result inevitably falls short of any convincing religious mysticism. The poems, to mark their seriousness, are composed in alexandrines, though with Romains's system of partial rhymes and *accords*. In general, we receive the impression that he is taking Unanimism too seriously, and the result is somewhat empty rhetoric. There are nevertheless individual poems where he achieves a more genuinely personal form of expression, in harmony with the Unanimist outlook, when he uses his experience of the joys of cycling—repeated in *Les Copains* —as a means of solidarity with the Village:

> *La fin du jour est belle et j'ai couru longtemps;*
> *La bicyclette osseuse a pourchassé les routes;*
> *L'air qu'elle déchirait tremble encore à ses roues;*
> *Et la fatigue est la couronne de mes tempes.*[25]

The most provocative expression of Unanimist ideas is to be found in *Manuel de Déification* (1910). This short work consists of a loosely linked series of precepts, some only a sentence or two in length, but others developed more fully, which, taken as a whole, were intended to form a recipe for the creation of Unanimist *dieux*. A literary ancestor of this form may be seen in Gide's *Nourritures terrestres*, though Romains's precepts are more restrained than Gide's ecstatic call to freedom. (The *Manuel* was composed precisely while he was in closest contact with Gide and the nascent *N. R. F.* group.) In any event, it is one of his works with which he proved least satisfied: he never allowed it to be reprinted, and though he has praised its *style nerveux et sobre*, he at the same time noted that its ideas were *propres à irriter un homme raisonnable*. These *formules de l'unanimisme militant, dans sa phase quasi religieuse*[26] in fact expressed clearly Romains's own feelings and sensibility at this time; and as in the case of the *Nourritures*, the inspiration is principally that of sublimated religious ardor. The preface makes clear that the *Manuel* should provide a form of compensation for empty lives of sadness, boredom, or bitterness. By an effort of will and intuitive powers, the reader of the *Manuel* will be able to merge himself into the collectivity, initially suggested as the city, but later more specifically as a group of human beings. The concept of the animator quickly rises to the surface, together with the *canular*:

> *Arrachez parfois les groupes à leur torpeur. Faies-leur violence . . . .*
> *Entrez dans une réunion publique; écoutez l'orateur, et soudain poussez*
> *un cri qui fasse mieux exister la salle . . . . C'est ainsi que tu déifieras les*
> *groupes rudes, plantant ton âme en leur centre, comme le drapeau sur la*
> *citadelle.*[27]

The situation then becomes one of violence, of the domination of the passive group by the animator: *Il te faudra ou le consentement ou la soumission d'autres hommes.*[28] Thus the group may become a *dieu*, the height of Unanimist activity; the note of exaltation perhaps even recalls Rimbaud:

> *Le jour où tous les hommes d'un groupe penseront à la même minute et de toute leur âme que leur groupe existe, le temps nouveau sera commencé.*[29]

But this mystical enthusiasm implies power over other human beings, even contempt for them:

> *Enorgueillis-toi de ta puissance. Tu disposes à ton gré de la vie des hommes . . . dis-toi que chaque homme du groupe, au prix de toi, n'est pas plus que ton orteil ou ton cheveu.*[30]

Another twist makes this readiness to accept violence revolutionary in nature:

> *Sois prêt aux plus brusques dieux. Ne sois pas de ceux qui tremblent au jour de l'émeute . . . . S'il te faut choisir, préfère encore le feu et l'explosion.*[31]

Romains ends by an irrational call to faith in Unanimism, despite the doubts of reason: *Si tu doutes de l'unanime, crée-le,*[32] and is prepared to accept that his precepts will only be followed by a small élite, but this will be sufficient justification.

It is difficult today to take the *Manuel* seriously as an ethical guide, as it is to accept the *Nourritures* as more than a passionate justification of egoistic sensuality. Indeed, Romains's precepts here show most clearly the barrenness and inconsistency of the Unanimist credo. Far from worshipping the collectivity as superior to the individual, he is in fact glorifying the individual—and one individual, himself—to whom everything else, things and human beings alike, must become subservient. The *unanime* will simply be formed by the immediate surroundings, in terms of people, of the all-important individual. In this light, Romains's Unanimism may be seen as simply an offshoot of Barrès's *culte du moi* and a vague Nietzschean feeling of the superior individual, which together provide, precisely, the primary inspiration of the *Nourritures*.

Romains takes up the theme of the *promenade* in *Un Être en marche* (1910). This volume contains two separate narrative poems, the title applying equally well to both. The first, subtitled *Poème épique*, treats the at first sight rather quaint theme of an outing by a *pension* of schoolgirls, formed into a crocodile and presenting an obvious *unanime*. The poet observes them setting off down the street to the station, boarding the train, dismounting in the country, walking through the fields, back to the train, the city, and the school again. The entire poem is narrated in the present tense as *poésie immédiate*, only immediate impressions and interrelationships being treated, without recourse to past events and above all to literary echoes. There is an unavoidable degree of artificiality in this technique, since the impressions recorded must either be imaginary or else the product of Romains's own walks near Paris, perhaps with Chennevière, but certainly not with a crocodile of schoolgirls. Equally, this group heroine is a little incongruous for a supposedly epic poem. But we do not need to view the poem as a demonstration of Unanimism or *poésie immédiate* to appreciate Romains's lively technical virtuosity. Hugo's *Djinns* is a precedent, on a smaller scale: sheer pleasure in metrical and rhythmical skill irrespective of meaning. Thus Romains uses a variety of meters—lines of from four to fourteen syllables—to attempt to represent content in the very form of his verse. As the girls move off down the street, he uses standard rhyme to indicate their regular movement, two by two, but as they pass a battalion, short snappy lines of four syllables illustrate the stamping of the soldiers' nailed boots. We may suspect Romains of concealing a smile when talking about the railway booking hall:

> *Le hall, bulle gonflée au souffle de la ville.*[33]

with deliberately exaggerated alliteration, or when he confronts the *unanime* of the girls with another, at first apparently more powerful, *unanime* of a flock of geese approaching them. His images are again deliberately striking: the poplars along the canal are like a caterpillar on its back with its legs in the air; or the train:

> *Le train dépasse un pont de fer*
> *Qui lui exaspère l'échine*
> *De son frôlement trop léger.*[34]

The second piece, *Poème lyrique*, is again narrated in the present, but here it is the poet himself who relates his *promenade*. He leaves his house, goes down the street to the crossroads, and walks around the city; the theme is the semimystical exaltation and feeling of intuitive "possession" of the things and people he sees:

> *Je suis à moi seul*
> *Le rythme et la foule*
> *Je suis les danseurs*
> *Et les hommes saouls.*[35]

The aim is to create a new kind of poetic sensibility, but although the idea is less artificial than in the *Poème épique*, the pattern is more confused. Perhaps the *Poème lyrique* might be compared with other spiritual journeys such as Baudelaire's *Voyage* or Rimbaud's *Bateau ivre*, but this very comparison points up the lack of intensity of Romains's poem. As a poetic entity, it is less successful than the *Poème épique*, and tends in part simply to repeat avenues already explored in *La Vie Unanime*.

VI *Unanimism on the Stage*

Romains's first play, *L'Armée dans la Ville*, on which he had worked since 1908, was performed in March, 1911, and published the same year. Its reception was a little stormy—a faint echo of the "battle" of *Hernani*?—largely because of its uncompromising Unanimism. In any case, Romains was well aware of the value of controversy in publicity, and a deliberately arrogant tone marks the play's preface. He makes blunt and sweeping affirmations, rather than indulging in rational argument. There has been no great dramatic art in France since the failure of Hugo's *Burgraves* in 1845; Symbolist drama has proved unsuitable for the stage; Rostand and Richepin offer no more than degraded Romantic drama; Moréas's imitation of classical tragedy is lifeless and insipid, while the drama of ideas is little better. So, to replace all these, Romains proposes his own formula: a simple drama, stripped of artifice, designed to be staged, not read, with a modern subject of general appeal. The action will rise to a crisis, and religious emotions will be roused in the audience through spiritual profundity. In addition, the drama will treat groups rather than individuals. In the past the only group really treated on the stage was the couple; now wider syntheses are needed, and the isolated individual is no more than an outdated convention. Furthermore, the highest dramatic art requires the medium of verse, which, since the resources of traditional prosody have become exhausted, while *vers libres* are too loose for the theater, must follow Romains's own model. To terminate, Romains mentions three poets approvingly: Claudel, Maeterlinck, and Verhaeren, while declaring his cult not only of Racine and Shakespeare, but also Aeschylus, Corneille, Goethe, and Hugo— thus implying that his own work will belong to the highest universal classical tradition.[36]

Prefaces are self-justificatory rather than explanatory, and we must judge *L'Armée* by its own qualities, not by the claimed ideal. In five acts, it presents the struggle between a city and its occupying Army. The exposition takes place in a café, where after ten months of oppression, a group of civilians plot to revolt against the soldiery, whose morale is breaking down with rivalry between infantry and cavalry. The soldiers reunite in face of the civilian threat and the act ends with an almost Romantic tirade celebrating the Army's earlier victory. In Act II, we see the General forcing his men back into a disciplined group, when the Mayor arrives with invitations for each soldier. The plot is that when these invitations are accepted, the citizens will all kill the individual soldier invited to their homes. Act III introduces the Mayor's wife, an altogether more determined personality, who admires the General but wishes his death; she exhorts a further group of women to sleep with the soldiers to make it easier to kill them later. In Act IV, the citizens hesitate, though their women urge them on hysterically. The Mayor's wife searches out the General, who has seen through the plot, but, weary of the horrors of war, is not prepared to take countermeasures, come what will. The struggle reaches its climax in the final act. The Mayor is pledged to kill the General at midnight, but when the moment arrives, dares not. His wife appeals to his patriotism without effect, then taunts him that she loves the General; now through jealousy, the Mayor shoots him. But the general plot has failed, and the Army is about to react bloodily, as the General dies. The Mayor's wife realizes her taunt has become true; she does indeed love the General.

The germ of the play is to be found in Romains's own experience on May 1, 1906, when his unit was ordered to Paris to prevent labor disorders, but literary sources can also be detected. There is a parallel with *Horace*,[37] while the Mayor's wife's love for the General is precisely Cornelian *amour-estime*. A play with a more direct influence is Hebbel's *Judith und Holofernes* (1840), also a five-act tragedy, where Judith murders Holophernes after sleeping with him.[38] Nevertheless, the play as it stands shows great originality and self-confidence. Its verse form follows Romains's precepts, with lines principally of eight, ten, or twelve syllables, based on *accords*. These yield striking effects, as in the drinking scene in Act I: *foule/ filles/feuilles/futailles/bouteilles/mille/ennemis*. The ·plot justifies its claim of being simple in structure, rising to a climax, with a modern subject. After French experiences in two World Wars, the play's appeal seems broad, but the lack of general appeal proved an obstacle to the play when performed: how far could the 1911 audience actually identify with the dramatic struggle? The citizens, when referred to, have French names such as Marguerite or Jean; the troops have mostly German ones, but not exclusively, as some too are French. It is doubtful whether Romains really wished to identify the City with France and the Army with Germany despite this indication, which may have merely confused the audience: doubtful because a careful balance is struck between the opposing sides, and the final issue is quite open until the end.

As Unanimist drama, *L'Armée* portrays the formation and disintegration of a series of groups, but comments are necessary. The sheer confines of the stage oblige smaller groups to substitute for the entire Army or the citizens, and in these groups it is on the Mayor's wife, the General, and the Mayor himself that dramatic interest is concentrated, as animators. The love theme in Act V has to be on the individual, not the collective plane. And once more, Unanimism implies violence. Naturally, dramatic tension must, whatever its expression, be caused by struggle, but it appears as if in practice Unanimism can get no further than animating mutually antagonistic groups: the social energy generated by the formation of a group needs to be directed against outsiders or other groups in an ultimately violent form. Implicit, too, is the idea that autocracy is more efficient than democracy, and that force is its own justification; the political implications of this may have disturbed Romains's audience more than himself.

In actual performance, the play made more demands on them than could be met. The verse form leads to a degree of stylization, despite brilliant passages, while some longer speeches are over-rhetorical. Elsewhere the necessity for verse seems slight. The use of groups makes the play seem abstract, and since the situation could not easily be assimilated to real life, verisimilitude is lacking. So is local color, and artificiality cannot be denied. Apollinaire, inspired by Gide, critized the play savagely, claiming that it loses all humanity and that Romains was treating a tragic subject with the means and the crude psychology of historical melodrama.[39] Doubtless this is excessive, but it points to genuine weaknesses in the play, which must however retain its place in literary history as an intriguing attempt at renewing poetic tragedy.

The *Premier livre de Prières* was reprinted as the second part of *Odes et Prières* in 1913. The *Odes* in the first part have been described by Romains as the first of his poems, except for a few pages of *La Vie Unanime*, which still have his complete approval. With their simplicity and directness, they realize his ambition to provide snatches of interior music which a man of today could recite to himself in the course of his day.[40] Written in 1911, the *Odes* are the least evidently Unanimist of Romains's early poems. Composed entirely in short lines of six, seven, or eight syllables, grouped in four-line stanzas, they are highly personal, communicating the poet's feelings, sometimes of simple joy, but more often of melancholy and unhappiness. Romains seems, indeed, at this period of his life, to have been obsessed with death, even suicide, and this theme haunts the collection:

> *Et tandis que la nue expire*
> *Un long cri pareil au brouillard,*
> *Je chancelle, pris à la nuque*
> *Par la détresse de mourir.*[41]

Although several of the poems seem to be addressed either to Gabrielle, shortly to become his wife, or to a friend (Chennevière?), in general a note of solitude prevails. Thus the poet sets out, alone, to climb a mountain in the Velay, or meditates in his room in Paris at night. Objects seem closer to him than people; the iron bed in his room, the whistling of trains, or

> *Le couteau dans une poche,*
> *La montre à côté du cœur.*
>
> *Je les tâte, je les serre,*
> *Je les possède en entier,*
> *Je les ajoute à ma chair*
> *Par un effet de l'amour . . .*[42]

Nostalgia for childhood adds a further dimension to melancholy. When the volume was republished in 1922, one of the *Odes* was suppressed, in which the poet expresses his hate for Sunday crowds, like Rimbaud and, later, Sartre. No doubt the irrational violence of his reactions was the cause of this removal:

> *Je calcule un coup de pied*
> *Cassant les familles raides.*
>
> *Ou plutôt, comme l'obus,*
> *Avoir la tonnante joie*
> *D'être, au centre de la foule,*
> *Un éclatement qui tue.*[43]

Reading the *Odes*, we feel that Romains's inspiration proceeds directly from his own feelings, not from any artificial Unanimist conceit. Unanimist ideas are still present, but in no way obtrude, and the result is a collection of individual lyrics universal in their appeal. The *Odes* provide, indeed, the easiest means of approaching Romains's poetry, and several of them have become well-known anthology pieces.

VII   Mort de quelqu'un

Romains's first long piece of fiction, and his early prose work generally most highly regarded, is *Mort de quelqu'un*, written in 1908–1910 and published in 1911. Here Romains, using Unanimist insights, succeeds in writing a novel displaying considerable originality both of theme and of technique. The theme of death was of course, in itself, nothing new in literature: Cuisenier has suggested Zola's *Mort d'O. Bécaille* and Tolstoy's *Death of Ivan Ilyitch* as works which might have influenced Romains,[44] though many other novels could have served equally well; to name Zola, *La Joie de vivre* might appear a likelier candidate, while Anatole France's *Histoire comique* is mostly devoted, in a different vein, to the consequences of the hero's death on those who outlive him. Where Romains's originality emerges is in his treatment of the theme: the physical aspect of death is sharply played down, while most of the novel treats its effects on the relatives and acquaintances of the dead man, ending with a mystico-philosophical monologue on death by an unnamed young man.

The title of the English translation, *Death of a Nobody*, perhaps does not accurately convey the nuance of the French; the protagonist, Jacques Godard, is not quite a mere "nobody," although he occupies a fairly low station in life as do practically all those who know him—the "humble" as Romains was to describe them in *Les Hommes de Bonne Volonté*. Godard, a childless widower, is a retired engine driver living in a small apartment in Northeast Paris;

he was originally from the Velay, where his parents still live, now in their eighties. Leading a simple life, one day he is struck by the idea that, after thirty-five years in Paris, he has never seen the view from the Panthéon, which he is now passing. Climbing the dome—incidentally one of Romains's own favorite viewpoints while at Normale, which with its panorama of the metropolis contributed to the Unanimist vision—he ironically catches a chill, which turns to pleurisy and fever, and dies some ten days later, without more suffering than annoyance at being incapacitated. To use Existentialist terminology, Godard's death is "absurd": contingent, without philosophical necessity. This is the "trigger," comparable to the scribbled sentences in *Le Bourg régénéré*, which sets in motion a series of Unanimist phenomena; a more vivid image would be the ripples on the surface of a pool, still moving long after the stone which caused them has sunk to the bottom. Godard is dead, but indirectly continues to exist in the consciousness of others as they hear about and reflect on his death. First the *concierge* finds the body, and has to cable Godard's parents and make the legal declaration, besides passing on the news to tenants and acquaintances. They, to the extent they actually knew Godard, find their consciousness altered by the news: small Unanimist groups are formed, such as the tenants who gain a new feeling of solidarity by jointly purchasing a wreath for the funeral. Meanwhile the telegram has reached Godard's parents, and his aged father sets off on the long journey to Paris, the first section on foot, then by stagecoach to the railway, then sitting up all night in the train. Other groups are formed: the passengers in the coach, those in the train, and the news of Godard's death takes on significance even for people who had never heard of him. At the funeral ceremony another Unanimist group is formed, while the procession to the cemetery takes up the image of the *rassemblement* once more: as it passes, even a violent struggle between strikers and police is temporarily quelled.

After the funeral, memories of Godard begin to fade. He is still occasionally remembered by former colleagues, by the Velay Association of which he had been a member—and by the *concierge* of his apartment block, no longer with a feeling of self-importance, but anxiety as he reflects on his own increasing age and infirmity. Godard died in the Spring, and during the next Winter is followed first by his mother, then his father, again quietly and simply. Almost a year after Godard's death, no more than vague fleeting recollections of him still exist: the young man can remember a funeral the previous Spring, but can get no nearer to the dead man's name than Boulard or Bonnard. Now Godard is truly dead, and the novel could well stop at this point; aesthetically, it might be improved. But the young man, evidently Romains himself, or at least Bénin of the later *Copains* (he mentions Broudier), feels the need to examine the concept of death, not so much by means of abstract analysis as by *connaissance immédiate*. He moves from this to a keen perception of the presence of life, which we may contrast with Existentialist reflections on existence: where Roquentin in *La Nausée* is negative, horrified by the contingency of existence, the young man is positive, optimistic to the point almost of denying death, because the individual, in a sense, survives in the mind of others. But this mood does not last: Godard is now forgotten by all who knew him—and the young man had never even seen him in the flesh. Perhaps a kind of superhuman effort could be made to resuscitate the dead—the young man sees himself as possessing a superior lucidity and vision—but he knows that he will in fact never achieve this miracle. He will continue to live, like everyone else, until some evening he too will have died.[45] With these words the book ends and the philosophical problem of mortality is, inevitably, left wide open.

Mort de quelqu'un is a considerable *tour de force*. The Unanimist elements, though omnipresent, do not jar: the formation of the group in the stagecoach, for example, around Godard's father, is in itself an admirable piece of economical prose, forming part of the general evocation of Velay life. Little trace remains of the earlier tendency to preach. Romains's style is in general sober and restrained, though occasionally illuminated by striking poetic images. Behind the theme of death lies a constant stress on spirituality, deepening what one can only call the tragic impact of the novel. There are, too, hints of telepathy, dreams, the power of will, and an obvious Bergsonian reference to the nature of time, all serving to link the book to the recurrent mystical strain in Romains, but again without undue emphasis. However, his greatest originality is in the creation of a novel without an active hero: an "antinovel" long before the coining of that term. With this is combined the technique of "simultaneity," already used in *Le Bourg régénéré*: here in the successive description of the various tenants' reactions to the thought of Godard's death. This technique foreshadows the famous "presentations" of *Les Hommes de Bonne Volonté*. Since *Mort de quelqu'un* was rapidly translated into English, Romains indeed claimed that it had great influence on literature in Britain and the United States,[46] and it is true that a similar technique of simultaneity is used by Dos Passos, among others. This may be a parallel rather than an influence, but in either case it underlines the originality of the novel; in the last half century, of course, simultaneity has been so frequently used as to become hackneyed. With *Mort de quelqu'un*, Romains again succeded in pioneering new ground; it was easily his most effective prose work to date.

VIII   Puissances de Paris

With *Puissances de Paris*, also published in 1911, Romains moves to a series of evocative short sketches on places and aspects of Paris, all perceived as *unanimes*. These are divided into groups: I. *Les Rues*; II. *Les Places*; III. *Les Squares*; IV. *Les Métamorphoses*; V. *Les Éphémères*; VI. *Les Vies intermittentes*; VII. *Réflexions*. There are no fictional plots, the unity between the individual sketches being provided by the group personality of the place portrayed; but Unanimist theory does not overweigh the purely artistic qualities of the book. French novelists have often tended to dwell lovingly on the topographical details of their capital: the tradition runs from Balzac through Flaubert and Zola right down to Simenon at the present day, and Romains was later to write a preface to the *Nagel Guide to Paris*. *Puissances de Paris* may indeed also be treated as a series of prose poems on Paris, with Baudelaire's *Spleen de Paris* as its ancestor; closer in time, parallels may be drawn too with Verhaeren, or Léon-Paul Fargue's early prose poems.

The first three sections deal with selected places in Paris, some well known like the Rue Royale, others less so like the passages between the Grands Boulevards and the Rue du Faubourg Montmartre. Throughout, the emphasis is on the busy life of streets and squares, not as inanimate settings but as part of the city's Unanimist existence. The most ambitious is the sketch of the Rue Montmartre, with the different groups of people who animate it at various times of day: 8:30 A.M., noon, 12:30, 3 P.M. and 10 P.M. The precise technique by which Romains gives life to these streets and squares is once again largely through personification: thus Rue Montmartre is like a woman with a headache. Certain places chosen show Romains's predilections, such as Place de l'Europe, the trains chugging beneath; the poetry of machinery also comes to the fore in the best of the fourth section, the *Métamorphoses*, the sketch on *L'Omnibus*, which moves from the bus company office, to the lineup waiting for the bus, its interior once the passengers have boarded, and the *impériale*, the open upper deck. The second metamorphosis recalls the *Ode à la Foule qui est ici:* Romains evokes the audience at the Opéra-Comique: the people waiting to enter, then the "birth of the house," and finally the "adult house," once the audience has developed full collective consciousness. *Les Éphémères* are based on similar ideas: the crowd at the cinema, or at the trick cyclist act at the circus; while in *Les Vies intermittentes* we see the *unanime* of the team of workers building the Métro, the bookstores in the Galeries de l'Odéon, the Sorbonne library, and a literary salon—this last the only sketch in the book where Romains departs from the otherwise constantly lyrical tone and indulges in irony.

The final section of *Réflexions* is very different, acting more as a postface than as an integral part of an artistic whole. Here Romains explains what he has been doing, in a distinctly didactic and slightly pretentious tone, explaining Unanimist theory once more. Intuition is stressed as the crucial means of perception: we must learn to know the groups around us not through external observation, but through organic consciousness.[47] Exactly how this process is to take place remains far from clear, and the suspicion arises once again that, in the last analysis, Romains's Unanimism is precisely an "individual dream" and, philosophically speaking, a self-contradiction. This is reinforced by a later remark, "I am addressing groups, those whose flesh I am,"[48] where we may reverse the terms and instead of taking the poet as the embodiment of the *unanime*, envision the *unanime* as a projection of the creative imagination of the poet. In practice Romains's Unanimistic technique is sustained by little more than repeated personification together with a search for the telling poetic image to bolster his enthusiastic vision of different Parisian groups. Keen observation and skillful descriptive abilities underlie the finished sketches just as much as in, say, Zola's Parisian descriptions in *Au Bonheur des Dames* or *Pot-Bouille*, while the total effect is perhaps not too far from the impressionism Romains claimed to abhor. The book contains some fine writing, but leads to a dead end: concentration on groups means that human interest is lacking and there is an instructive contrast here with *Mort de quelqu'un*, which is equally in accordance with Unanimist theory but where the group and the individual are well balanced. Romains has evolved a useful technique but tried to make it an end in itself; in *Les Hommes de Bonne Volonté* there are many similar passages, but they tend to form an integral part of the general narrative texture of the novel rather than standing alone.

IX   Les Copains

The next of Romains's prose works was *Les Copains*, first published in 1913 and reprinted countless times since; a film version appeared in 1964. Totally different from *Mort de quelqu'un* in tone and theme, it is a gay, farcical story which has given such pleasure to successive generations that it seems almost churlish to submit it to literary analysis. The "pals" of the title are seven in number, all students: Bénin, Broudier, Huchon, Lamendin, Lesueur, Martin, and Omer; at the start of the book they are finishing a well-lubricated meal in a bistro. Bénin, expelled from the room for a joke which ends in spilling wine on the others, finds a dusty attic and leads the way there; among other junk is a map of France, where two names strike their eyes: Ambert and Issoire (actual small towns, in central France). The group sees these towns as a challenge, and promptly has a competition to write a poem on the rhymes: Issoire, Ambert, Passoire and Camembert, with a set of amusing pastiches as the result. The group then moves to see a "somnambulist" with mediumistic powers, who, oracle-like, produces a short poem in couplets for them, hinting at what further "vengeance" they should take on Ambert and Issoire.

We next accompany Bénin and his bicycle by train to Nevers, where, passing himself off as an important Russian official, he makes a speech in Latin, duly translated by Broudier in a ceremony at the station, complete with playing of the *"Marseillaise"* and the Russian national anthem. The same night the two set off cycling toward Ambert, where they eventually meet the others at the circular town hall at midnight. There the "vengeance" begins with the "creation of Ambert": Broudier, attired in false beard and top hat, masquerading as a Minister with a suite of officials, has the colonel of the garrison and his two battalion commanders awakened in the middle of the night and sets the troops off on a series of crazy maneuvers. Bugle calls and shots shatter the nocturnal silence, the terrified inhabitants rush into the streets: Ambert now exists. The following Sunday it is Bénin's turn in "le rut d'Ambert": metamorphosed into Père Lathuile, the famous theologian, he is invited by the parish priest to preach the morning sermon, which he does on the theme of impurity, exhorting his flock to the maximum of sexual connection, whether inside or outside the marriage bond. By the end of the sermon the men—inspired by the example of three of the *copains*—are making sexual assaults on the nearest women, largely unresisted. Next comes the turn of Issoire. Here a statue of Vercingétorix, the Celtic leader against Julius Caesar, has been planned for some time: the plot of land in the square has been set aside, a pedestal erected, and even a bronze horse acquired, so that only the hero himself is lacking. A young sculptor from Paris has offered, gratis, to present the statue, and we see the opening ceremony, with every dignity and pompous speechifying from local worthies. But the statue, when unveiled, proves to be Bénin once more, stark naked, who interrupts the speechmaking, abuses the crowd and throws potatoes at them. This is the "destruction" of Issoire, with the crowd, even the military band and escort, fleeing in terror. The book ends with another joyful repast at a house in the forest, with a dozen bottles of wine disappearing in shouts and laughter.

Les Copains is very much a young man's novel, in conception dating back to Romains's years at Normale; by the time of publication he was married and had been a philosophy teacher for four years. The actual writing of the book was mostly done during Romains's regular train journeys from Paris to Laon, where he was teaching from 1910; but the seven *copains* have their models in the group of Romains's friends of several years earlier: Broudier is Chennevière, Lesueur is Vildrac, Huchon with his thick spectacles, Duhamel, and Bénin (who plays the largest part in the book) Romains himself.[49] The unfortunate towns of Ambert and Issoire were not simply chosen at random, but had been visited by Romains during a cycling expedition. However, the *canulars* perpetrated on the two towns belong to wish fulfillment rather than reality (and, with the somnambulist episode, are not particularly plausible on sober examination). For the rest, the general tone is that of the student community: a mixture of highly colloquial language (a heritage of Naturalism) and pseudo-erudite pomposity: Bénin's speech in Latin, or the *bouts-rimés*, together with numbers of scatological jokes and a tendency towards facetiousness by the third person narrator.

Unanimist preoccupations pervade *Les Copains*, which in this respect is a direct development not of *Mort de quelqu'un*, but of *Le Bourg régénéré*. The whole idea of "creating" Ambert and "destroying" Issoire are no more than an elaborate version of "regenerating" the *bourg*: the collectivity, initially passive (its original sin) has to be stirred to dynamic activity. This time the animators are nominally a group though in fact Bénin is clearly their own animator, but again we have the contrast between provincial small-town torpor and violent awakening from the metropolis. (The moral implications of farce rarely yield much edification, and the *rut d'Ambert* episode in particular is on the point of becoming a mass rape when the narration ceases.) One of the most interesting passages in the novel, from the viewpoint of ideas, is Bénin's final speech, admittedly when well wined: here he praises the *copains* for having restored the *Acte Pur*, the *Arbitraire Pur*, in the tradition of Alexander, Attila, and Napoleon. The key passage is worth quoting:

> *Vous avez, sans ombre de raison, enchâiné l'un à l'autre des actes gratuits.*
> *Vous avez établi entre les choses les rapports qui vous agréaient . . .*
> *Vous ne vous êtes asservis à quoi que ce fût, fût-ce à vos propres fins.*[50]

Here we have, in the year before Gide's *Les Caves du Vatican*, a clear definition of the *acte gratuit*, and it is difficult not to accept that Gide was considerably indebted to him, not only for the idea of the *acte gratuit* but also for the very form of *Les Caves*: the *sotie*—a term which applies equally well to *Les Copains*. At the same time, Romains's definition here shows another of the roots of Unanimism: the imposition of the individual will, even arbitrary, on things and *autrui*. We may, if we wish, see here an anticipation of the ideas of Malraux and Sartrean Existentialism, that the individual can create his own essence or destiny; though for Romains there remains an element of mysticism. And the deification of the group is explicit: *Je te salue donc, ô dieu unique, par tes sept noms, Omer, Lamendin, Broudier, Bénin, Martin, Huchon, Lesueur.*[51]

All the principal comic episodes can be viewed as Unanimist set pieces, but at the same time the satirical attitudes lying behind them are stereotypes. In Bénin's hoax on the Ambert garrison, we can see Romains's own vengeance on the idiocies inflicted on him during his military service; but antimilitarism, comic or otherwise, had already a literary ancestry dating back at least to the 1880's. Similarly the satire in Father Lathuile's sermon is traditional, while the whole idea of mocking the benighted provincial petty bourgeoisie is a stock post-Romantic attitude: *Madame Bovary* is far from the only parallel. The comic mechanism of the *canular* here depends once more on the credulity of the passive mass, manipulated by the more cunning individual to his own advantage, though the farcical context again conceals the potentially dangerous consequences of Unanimist action. Even the apparent unanimity of the seven *copains* is an illusion, maintained artificially by alcoholic exhilaration. True friendship, rather than comradeship, involves a more genuine exchange of confidence, and this is only seen in Bénin and Broudier talking while they cycle towards Ambert, especially where Broudier, in serious tone, sees friendship as, above all, a means of defeating his metaphysical solitude and fear of death. This is followed by Bénin's evocation of a privileged moment one day when the pair had been walking round Paris. Here the novel attains its most serious level, completely different from the joyful tone of carefree comedy so brilliantly sustained elsewhere.

X   *The Eve of War*

Following *Les Copains* came *Le Vin blanc de La Villette*, published in May, 1914, under the title of *Sur les Quais de La Villette*, Romains restored his original title when the work was brought out again by the *N.R.F.* in 1923. The book consists of a dozen prose sketches, a loosely linked series of anecdotes supposed to have been told or heard by Bénin and Broudier at a bar in La Villette, frequented by bargemen and stevedores, on the canal in industrial Northeast Paris. Several of these sketches had been published separately in reviews. Three have an autobiographical basis; Romains's experience of *La Prise de Paris* in April, 1906, when his infantry regiment was sent to Paris in readiness against the threatened general strike of May 1. This was indeed the most powerful experience of Romains's military service, when the troops marched through Paris like an occupied city, completely dominating the civilian population and averting the strike. The tone is one of uncritical admiration for military force, a dream of violence with no moral inhibitions, and war itself as a pleasant prospect. We should note that the inspiration here is essentially antirevolutionary: the suppression of a movement of protest by sheer force.

Other anecdotes, however, are written from the opposite view-point, which equally appears to have Romains's approval. Thus, *Une simple promenade* describes the workers' May Day march of a year later, when they on their side instilled fear into bourgeois hearts by marching up the Champs-Élysées. The sketch was in fact reprinted by a Communist publication in 1925 as *un bel acte révolutionnaire.* [52] Other political anecdotes treat the execution of Ferrer, a now forgotten event in Spanish history, and the repression of the famous protest march in St. Petersburg in January, 1905. *La Charge des autobus* combines the idea of social revolution with the Unanimist *canular*, when a group of disenchanted bus drivers organize a charge down a wide street in North Paris. This episode has no factual basis, but brings home the idea of social violence as a kind of distraction for boredom. *Le Lynchage de la rue Rodier* shows two *apaches* terrorizing a Paris street, then spontaneously being lynched by the inhabitants; here there is, for once, no animator. Romains again appears to approve of this outcome, despite its violence, justifying it by uncritically placing the crowd above the individual. The last three sketches treat the power of human will. The protagonist is an *ancien maître des hommes*, who can hypnotize not only individuals, but also groups, who sleeps nine days through sheer autosuggestion and who, in a final feat, compels a man to enter a lion's cage in perfect safety since the lion itself is mesmerized and dominated. These sketches are doubtless imaginary; they indicate Romains's lasting interest and belief in the power of mind over matter, specifically the power of the human will.

The strongest impression created by the book is one of enthusiasm for power, whether social protest, repression of that same protest, of individuals who disturb group security, or finally domination of others through the mind. In most cases this represents the glorification of the group over the individual, without further differentiation —how else to reconcile *La Prise de Paris* with *Une simple promenade*? We may perhaps also detect here the influence of Georges Sorel's *Réflexions sur la violence*, while what we have is merely the most naked expression of a tendency already noted in Romains. Enthusiasm for Unanimism seems to have precluded moral judgment of its implications, and there is still a good deal of immaturity in Romains's treatment. Moreover, the farcical lightheartedness of *Les Copains* is absent from these sketches, which remain only as fragmentary curiosities of his early enthusiasms.

With Romains's works of the immediate prewar period we can group *Le Voyage des amants*, an extended poem dedicated to Gabrielle. Written in 1913–1914, it should have appeared in the latter year; however, outbreak of war delayed publication until 1920.[53] Once again, Romains's theme is that of a journey; this time a genuine journey made by himself and his wife to Amsterdam, shortly after their marriage. The volume consists of over thirty individual poems grouped into four sections: before the journey; the train trip through Belgium; Amsterdam; while in the last section, the poet links the actual journey with other memories, including the famous Unanimist vision in, precisely, the Rue d'Amsterdam. Romains manages to convey a keen sense of the real experience of traveling, like the weariness of changing trains, with an equally vivid evocation of its poetry. This latter is especially felt in the initial section, where the couple suddenly feel a sense of being cramped in Paris:

> *Quelque chose est absent qui était entre nous.*
> *L'espace merveilleux a fui comme un oiseau . . .*[54]

Inquiétude turns into *impatience*, and the poet recalls memories of previous travels, to Marseilles, and Brest. In the second section, Romains again is able to indulge his feeling for machinery: *Ode en Express* is a brilliant attempt to recapture the rhythmical rattling of the train over the rails:

> *Des chocs profonds*
> *Secouent*
> *La tête et les*
> *Entrailles*
>
> *Ce sont les roues*
> *Qui butent*
> *Contre le bout*
> *Des rails.*[55]

Once in Amsterdam, there is no artificial glamorization of experience; fatigue and irritability form part of the poet's subject matter, and also nostalgic memories of Paris: Montmartre and La Villette. In the last section, with the evocation of the vision in Rue d'Amsterdam, a coincidence giving the Dutch city a mystical aura, with memories of the Kalverstraat, the main street in Amsterdam, and a description of an imaginary sea journey from London to

Amsterdam, Romains moves away again from reality to the more ideal plane of journeying in the mind, thus bringing the theme full circle. As Romains comments, *Le Voyage des amants* can be taken as a kind of verse pendant to *Puissances de Paris*, but the delay in publication through the War made it seem something of an anti-climax to *Europe*, and weakened its impact.[56] Such chronological considerations naturally do not affect the reader today, who can appreciate Romains's poems for what they are, a remarkably precise evocation of the sensations, pleasant or tiresome, of travel.

CHAPTER 3

Years of Success

I *The War and its Aftermath*

THE outbreak of World War I in August, 1914, found Romains touring the Velay with his wife and some friends. Unfit for active service, he served as auxiliary until released in 1915 to teach at the Collège Rollin in Paris. He was doubly fortunate in this, as he not only was spared fighting in the holocaust, but with light duties, often not even in uniform, and with long spells of sick leave, he was able to pursue his literary work. In particular, he wrote the long poem *Europe*, and also worked on other poetry and his play *Cromedeyre*. In Fall, 1917, he moved to a post at Nice, which he held until he resolved to give up teaching as a career two years later.

The War shattered the carefree world of Romains's youth, permanently changing his views and preoccupations. His initial reaction was one of absolute horror at the unnecessary catastrophe which had overcome Europe, a stance far removed from the jingo patriotism of most Frenchmen. He fully supported Romain Rolland's denunciation of the War in *Au-dessus de la mêlée* (1915), and *Europe* (1916) contains some of his finest verse, eloquently expressing his emotion. An article written for publication in America, but which did not subsequently appear, is reproduced in *Problèmes d'aujourd'hui* and explains his position in detail. To voice such opinions required considerable moral courage at the time, and Romains showed a good deal of prescience in his reasoning, since his analysis of the War as a European Civil War, a useless tragedy which might bring about the downfall of civilized Western values, is widely accepted today. Moreover, it also led to a fundamental change in his attitude toward politics. Whereas he had been a Socialist sympathizer before 1914, content to watch events as a passive observer, he now determined to do his utmost, once the War was over, to ensure that it would never be repeated. This is at the basis of practically all his political activity in the 1930's, however misguided individual moves may now seem, and it may be compared with Sartre's later *engagement*, developing from a

similar feeling of guilt at prewar political detachment. This change
in attitude was not confined to public life: the entire series of
Les Hommes de Bonne Volonté is permeated with the obsession of
war, fear of it in the early volumes, war itself as the central theme
of the two Verdun books, often regarded as the finest, and afterwards, preservation of peace, growing more and more pessimistic
as the novel draws to its close.

At the War's end in 1918, Romains's literary career was more than
satisfactory for a man of his age, thirty-three. He had behind him
solid achievements: several volumes of poetry, a play and various
prose works, together with a considerable number of critical
articles and essays. Almost everything he had written bore the stamp
of originality. He was the acknowledged leader of a recognized
literary movement, Unanimism, his play had attracted wide notice
if not material success, there had been talk of the Goncourt
Prize for *Mort de quelqu'un*, and, not least, through a flair for
publicity, he had constantly kept his name before the public.
All this on top of a solid academic career. Nor had the War years
been barren, since he had been able to pursue his literary projects,
as well as scientific research on extraretinal vision. And he had found
himself a permanent publisher, Gaston Gallimard and the *N.R.F.*,
whereas before the War, he had been obliged to publish as and where
he could, often at his own expense. The importance of a writer's
publishing arrangements is too frequently ignored by critics, partly,
it is true, through lack of relevant information. Yet Proust, Gide,
and Martin du Gard were men fortunate in possessing private
means, whose literary careers could scarcely have developed in
the way they did if they had been obliged to earn a living, as was
the case for both Duhamel and Romains. Without the confidence
generated by a semipermanent contract with a reliable publisher,
the promising writer may hesitate to undertake a major project
which might make his name, and instead fritter away his creative
energies on minor journalism and other tasks for which there is
immediate if moderate financial return. Especially so if he has
family commitments, and an entire literary career may thus be
crippled: Chennevière is a case in point. His contract with the *N.R.F.*
in his pocket, Romains could face the future with optimism.
Duhamel at the same time was enabled to devote himself entirely
to literature through the enormous success of his War books, notably
the award of the Goncourt Prize to *Civilisation* in 1918.

Romains continued teaching at Nice after the Armistice, but fell victim to the Spanish influenza epidemic and was seriously ill through most of Winter, 1918–1919. What further energies he had at this time were devoted largely to extraretinal vision. Then he learned that in Fall, 1919, he was to be transferred to Amiens in Northern France, and not wishing to assume this post, he decided to take the plunge and abandon teaching. This was obviously running some risk since literary prestige alone does not guarantee prosperity, and in the meantime reduced his income considerably; which perhaps explains to some extent his dramatic projects in following years, since the theater is the literary sphere where success most quickly brings financial returns. With his enormous energy and appetite for work, however, Romains could now expect greatly to increase his production while maintaining absolute freedom. Always eager to explore new countries, he became one of France's most widely traveled writers, initially on an inexpensive basis as as a private individual, later, as his reputation soared, as an enthusiastic attender of conferences and honored literary guest. Thus he revisited Switzerland in late 1919, traveled extensively in Spain in 1920, and went to North Africa in the following year, visiting Tunisia and Morocco. The early interwar years saw the founding of the P.E.N. Club, an international association of writers dedicated to mutual understanding and freedom of expression. Romains was an early member and the P.E.N. Congress at New York in January, 1924, gave him his first glimpse of the United States. About the same time, he was becoming increasingly concerned about the maintenance of peace, and in 1925 and 1926 made warmly received speeches in Berlin on the necessity for Franco-German understanding. 1927 saw Romains in Austria and Finland, 1928 in Norway. Another visit to Austria took place in 1930, and a long tour of the Near East—Palestine, Egypt, and Syria—in 1931. This international travel was accompanied by several changes in residence in France itself. In 1920, he bought a small house at Hyères, near Toulon, where he lived and wrote—above all *Knock*—when not in Paris. Nine years later he would sell this house, together with a villa he had built in Paris, and buy a country estate, a sizeable house with attached vineyards, in Touraine. He also combined purely literary work with various journalistic tasks. He acted as poetry critic for the newspaper, *L'Humanité*, until it fell under Communist control; in 1927 he was special correspondent for

L'Illustration at the Beethoven centenary celebrations in Vienna; later he became a regular correspondent for *La Dépêche de Toulouse*. He also wrote a variety of essays, notably one on Freud, published in the *N.R.F.* in 1922. Two major events took place in Romains's private life during the same period. Georges Chennevière died in his early forties in August, 1927, thus ending Romains's closest friendship, of nearly thirty years' standing. And Romains's first marriage, which had begun under scarcely auspicious circumstances, gradually began to break down, as so often, after the husband's rise to fame. Final separation would take place in 1934, with a divorce two years later.

The most eloquent expression of Romains's attitude to war is to be found in his poem *Europe*, published at the very height of the struggle. The theme was one which had already tempted Romains before the War: the Continent as the supreme Unanimist group, and therefore *dieu*. However, the dream had turned into a nightmare, and the poems contained in the collection express Romains's horror at this totally unnecessary disaster. His patriotism does not imply exclusive Nationalism, and he sees himself a citizen of Europe just as much as he is of France:

> *L'Europe, mon pays, est en proie aux armées.*
> *Le continent grouille par terre, comme un sac*
> *De serpents enfumés qui s'éveillent et mordent.*
> *Des villes, au hasard, éclatent sous leurs dents.*

> *Et la France, par qui mon corps tient à l'Europe,*
> *Multitude où je trempe, et qui me continue,*
> *Terroir de mes pensées, terrain de ma tribu . . .*[1]

The initial cry of horror gives way to evocation of memories of the peaceful Europe of earlier years:

> *Un poteau frontière entre des pommiers en fleurs.*
> . . . .
> *Gai, luisant, neuf, et tout chatouillé de soleil*
> *À cause d'un vent doux qui remuait les feuilles.*[2]

Romains then returns to the struggle itself, making skillful use of fourteen-syllable lines:

> *La pluie tombe sur le cinq-centième jour de la guerre.*[3]

He shows the effect of war on the ordinary soldiers, whose only real desire is to recapture the simple pleasures of peacetime life.

The collection ends with an invocation to the *Foules de l'Europe vivante* not to allow their homeland—the entire Continent—to die, overwhelmed by violence, and to attempt to recreate the happiness of peaceful existence.

In *Europe*, Romains does much more than simply repeat the ideas of Romain Rolland, though indeed it is surprising that the poems passed the censorship. The experience of Unanimism has now come to maturity, and the naïve optimism of much of Romains's earlier work has given way to a tragic realization of the grimmer aspects of human life. His memories of youthful and innocent travels through Europe take on an added poignancy when they are shown in contrast with present horrors: a comparison with *Le Voyage des amants* makes this immediately clear. *Europe* is, without doubt, *poésie engagée*, but is also excellent literature in its own right, in which Romains succeeds in blending personal vision with universal events.

Another poetical work completed by Romains in 1916 was *Les Quatre Saisons*, four short poems published as a plaquette the following year. Here Romains turns away from the carnage of war and returns to the inspiration of Baudelaire's *Tableaux parisiens*, for he treats the seasons not in terms of a rustic Nature, but as they affect the bustling industrial city:

> *Derrière les docks et les gares,*
> *Dans un pays de murs aveugles,*
> *Un carrefour s'étire, pris*
> *À moitié sous un pont de fer.*[4]

These poems, evoking the stifling heat of summer or the sense of rejuvenation in spring, may be placed together with *Puissances de Paris* in their celebration of the capital.

II *Extraretinal Vision*

One of the strangest episodes in Romains's career, and one where the nonscientific layman treads at his peril, is his claimed discovery of "extraretinal," also sometimes called "paroptic," vision. This phenomenon, theoretically of enormous importance biologically, Romains maintained to have demonstrated beyond contradiction, but it was never accepted by the leading French scientists who observed his experiments; the outcome was a great bitterness against "official science" on Romains's part for the rest of his life.

Romains's interest in the possibility of a type of "sight" through other organs than the eyes went back to his student days, when he thought he observed something similar in fishes. As a trained scientist as well as a philosophy teacher, he continued this interest, especially after moving to Nice. By 1918 he had completed series of experiments to confirm the theories he was developing, and was working with soldiers blinded in the war. Later he used other subjects who this time were blindfolded. At this point Romains fell victim to Spanish influenza and had to interrupt his researches; early in 1919, he wrote to Duhamel announcing his discoveries, but although Duhamel arranged interviews with leading scientists, these came to nothing. Romains therefore published in 1920 a short monograph on his theories, *La Vision extra-rétinienne et le Sens paroptique*, his only work under the name of Louis Farigoule. Later that year he was invited to demonstrate his results at the Sorbonne; the professors attending were not convinced—nor, incidentally, was Duhamel, whose relations with Romains consequently cooled for some years. Romains stuck to his guns with new editions of his brochure, including an English translation, together with an account of similar work carried out by another philosophy teacher, René Maublanc.[5]

Romains's theory depends fundamentally on the belief that in the skin there exist minute organs which can not only pick up light images, but also transmit them to the brain. These he thought he had actually discovered, and named them *ocelles*. Suitable subjects might therefore be found who, while temporarily blindfolded and especially sensistive, would be able to distinguish visual shapes and colors by this means. The state of special sensitivity was achieved by means which appear to differ little from hypnotism, but which Romains described as the *delta régime*. What exactly happened at the Sorbonne experiments is now difficult to establish. Romains, writing later in a rancorous tone which reveals neither the objectivity of the scientist nor the detachment of the philosopher, simply accused those present of being blinded by prejudice and animosity. On the other side, no doubt suspicions of bad faith were also present—and Romains's reputation as author of *Les Copains* and notorious perpetrator of *canulars* was scarcely calculated to help him. Some were puzzled by his results but found his theories difficult to accept, falling back on the explanation that light was somehow getting through the blindfold. In 1923 Romains repeated the experiments before other scientists (and the aged Anatole France whose opinion he regarded as particularly valuable); regarding the phenomena and theory as established scientific facts, there he left them, claiming that he would be justified before long by research from Harvard to Yokohama, while the doubters would soon have their boat on the water when they saw how the wind was blowing.[6]

To date the matter has not in fact gone much further. Certain research, not specified in detail, is said to have borne out Romains's theories; on the other hand, knowledge of it has not filtered through to our own colleagues in biology, who have viewed the theory with the sort of skepticism that is the usual scientific reaction to extrasensory perception—with which indeed there is a parallel. The difficulty appears to be not so much a flat refusal to countenance the whole idea, but in accepting Romains's theory in detail. If the *ocelles* indeed exist, their presence in the skin ought to be demonstrable; but this has not been satisfactorily done. And although it is apparently true that the eye has in part evolved from skin cells, which might leave open the possibility of the skin itself possessing some sensory powers, the remainder of the eye belongs, biologically, to the brain. Even if the *ocelles* were to exist, the transmission and interpretation of light images would still be a mystery.

In a literary study, whether or not the theory of extraretinal vision is scientifically justified is not important. Right or wrong, it alters the literary value of his works not a whit. Nevertheless, his researches and his strong emotive reaction to their rejection do cast light on certain springs of his creative imagination, and on his ambitions as scientist as well as artist. Thus his desire to establish himself in virtually every field of literature, and as a major figure in science as well. Goethe, after all, spent much time and effort on scientific research, though he is not particularly remembered for his results, and perhaps, too, it is not entirely unfair to recall Hugo's obsession with table-rapping on Jersey. Duhamel, who much sooner than Romains became disabused with the facile optimism of materialistic science, but whose experience as doctor and researcher was considerably more extensive, is probably as sensible a guide as any. Although he did not accept Romains's theory, he did not think the whole affair was simply another mystification (and if it was, it backfired). Romains wished, he considered, to make some great scientific discovery through intuition and imagination. (So much for the soundness of the actual research.) He initially heard about the matter in a strange letter where Romains described himself as possessing "new powers," and he concluded that Romains, fascinated with the mysteries of life, wished to "colonize some new province of the unknown."[7]

This brings us to the other point. Consciously an anti-Romantic, deploring the excesses of unbridled individualism and seeing himself as representative of a new Classicism, Romains could not escape entirely—as who among us can?—Romantic attitudes. He placed the artist's calling at the highest level, and in his later political activities, too, there is the vision of the poet as prophet. Yet although displaying in many ways a levelheaded and robust common sense, there was a strong streak of irrationalism in him. Unanimism, as we have seen, is largely an intuitive, mystical doctrine. It is human will which, rationally explicable, brings about the *débâcle* of Ambert and Issoire in *Les Copains*, and which, irrationally, dominates the lion in *Le Vin blanc de La Villette*. The "new powers" Romains spoke of to Duhamel are reflected in several later books, but whether they form the strongest part of his work is another matter.

III   Cromedeyre *and* Donogoo

Immediately following production of *L'Armée dans la Ville*, Romains had set to work on another full-length verse drama, *Cromedeyre-le-Vieil*. However, with other projects under way and the interruption of the War years, the play was not completed until 1918, and was first performed at Jacques Copeau's Théâtre du Vieux-Colombier in May, 1920. Once again the subject of the play can be seen as a kind of demonstration of Unanimism, but now Romains has moved away from the abstract setting of *L'Armée dans la Ville* and chosen his native Velay as the scene. Cromedeyre, which acts as a group hero, is an imaginary village in the mountains, but other place names are perfectly genuine. The characters are no longer simply designated as First Infantryman or the Mayor's Wife, but have traditional peasant names such as Anselme, Mère Agathe, and Claude le Pêcheur.

Act I contains the exposition: we hear Cromedeyre described from the outside, at an inn further down the mountain. It resembles no other village, but it is much older, and its inhabitants have a sense of solidarity lacking elsewhere, combined with hostility towards outsiders. The houses are all built onto each other with internal connecting passages, and their church is unlike all other churches, with no tower, no bells, no altar, and no priest. They have indeed sent one of their young men, Emmanuel, to the seminary, with the idea that he shall become their priest, but, dissatisfied with the teaching, he has left and at the end of the act arrives at the inn on his way home. This is one of the two main themes in the play; the other lies in Cromedeyre's constant shortage of women, since more male children are born than girls. A century ago, the men of Cromedeyre carried off girls from other villages and kept them after a violent battle. Now the same situation is about to recur. In Act II, Emmanuel meets the *doyen* of the monastery, also on his way to Cromedeyre to bring the village back to religious orthodoxy, but when he realizes who Emmanuel is and the harsh reception he is likely to receive, he abandons his enterprise. The second tableau of Act II takes us to the Assembly of the Elders in Cromedeyre. The church has just been completed without diocesan assistance and a celebration is planned:

> ... *une dure orgie,*
> *Des épaisseurs de nourriture,*
> *Une colère de boissons,*
> *Une ivresse de tous les membres*
> *Qu'on met deux jours à ressuer ...* [8]

Emmanuel arrives, explaining that he has left the seminary and put the *doyen* to flight. He is going to be the means by which Cromedeyre once again asserts its individuality and its own religion —another aspect of the animator. As an immediate step, confession and penitence are to be suppressed. The act ends with a miracle as Emmanuel heals a sick child. The third act moves to the Laussonne valley down the mountain from Cromedeyre, where Emmanuel is talking to Thérèse, the shepherdess he loves. He hints that Cromedeyre may repeat its kidnapping of women and tells her not to be afraid. In Act IV, the kidnapping takes place, the scene being narrated entirely at second hand as Mère Agathe, a very old woman, has a clairvoyant vision and describes the events she "sees." Fifteen girls including Thérèse are carried off to Cromedeyre; but their terror is gradually stilled, and the act ends with Cromedeyre's victory in another pitched battle to defend its captives.

The girls are married in Act V in a pagan ceremony performed by Mère Agathe, who reveals she is in fact the last survivor of the earlier kidnapping, "a thousand moons ago." They are now reconciled to becoming members of the Cromedeyre collectivity, and when emissaries are sent up from Laussonne to beg them to return, they refuse. The play ends by reinforcing the same point on the supernatural plane; a cripple attempts to charm the girls back and seems on the point of succeeding when Emmanuel threatens him with a more powerful spell and the cripple, paralyzed by terror, is only too glad to escape.

The play has two obvious sources: a factual one in a genuine dispute in the Velay between parish and bishop about the right to name the priest,[9] and a literary one in the Rape of the Sabine Women. Romains has succeeded in combining these two disparate elements in a drama of considerably more power than *L'Armée dans la Ville*. Even hostile critics were impressed by its haunting poetic qualities and compelling evocation of atmosphere. Despite the Velay setting, *Cromedeyre* can in no sense be called a realistic play; although using elements of local color, and especially rustic dialect, Romains has created a closed world, dominated by ritual, and entirely imaginary, dependent even on supernatural elements. According to the stage directions, the action takes place "in our days," but there is nothing which attaches it to any age, and this gives it a timeless quality. What is presented is an idealized, if violent, pastoral existence somewhat similar to that shown in the early novels of Jean Giono ten years later. Despite its qualities, Cromedeyre only received a *succès d'estime*, which we cannot but regret since it deflected Romains from further attempts at poetic drama. Nor can he be blamed for this, as a playwright more than any other type of writer requires practical success in order to continue. Perhaps it is impossible to revive the verse drama as an artistic form with the prestige of its Classical forebears, but *Cromedeyre* is nevertheless highly original both in conception and in execution, more so indeed than Romains's later theatrical successes.

What probably detracted from the play's appeal is what immediately strikes the present-day reader: the glorification of harshness and violence. If considerations of form and style are put aside, what we are left with is simply the ritualistic celebration of a tribe, whose greater "racial purity" and aggressiveness enable it to indulge in robbery and rapine not only without punishment, but with evident approval. The uneasy fascination with violence which we have seen in so many of Romains's earlier works seems now to have turned into unrestrained endorsement. Once more the group seems to exist only in opposition to other groups, in this case less well knit and effective, and once more Unanimist doctrine leads to violent struggle in short order. And although, following the precepts of the *Manuel de Déification*, we are shown the creation of a *dieu*, the vision contains totalitarian elements, combined with regression to a more primitive and savage level of culture. The idea of "might is right" becomes quite explicit:

> *Cromedeyre est une chair unique*
> *Qui se perpétue, crochée au sol.*
> *Il accumule dans sa personne*
> *Beaucoup d'orgueil, beaucoup de malice,*
> *Beaucoup de haine et de fourberie.*
> . . . .
> *Cromedeyre saisit avec tant de force*
> *La chair étrangère dont il a besoin*
> *Qu'elle coule en lui comme du vin d'airelles.*[10]

But perhaps it is making too much of what is after all no more than a work of fantasy, Romains's poetic imagination playing on his knowledge of the Velay mountain villages, to see in *Cromedeyre* no more than a blueprint for totalitarian society. As a poetic drama, the play deserves attention no less than the earlier work of Rostand and Maeterlinck.

Shortly after the end of World War I, the poet Blaise Cendrars, then active in films, invited Romains to write him a script. Tempted by the opportunity to work in a new medium, Romains set about a kind of sequel to *Les Copains*, but, as so often happens, the film project fell through. Having completed his scenario, however, Romains published it in 1920 under the title of *Donogoo-Tonka, ou les Miracles de la Science*. Several earlier works would seem to be eminently filmable: *Le Rassemblement, Le Bourg régénéré*, and of course a film of *Les Copains* eventually was made; indeed, the whole idea of animating groups seems to be closely akin to well-known cinematographic techniques. Bearing in mind that in 1920 the film as an art form was in its infancy, Romains's scenario appears remarkably well adapted to the silent cinema, with its elaborate mime, wide-ranging settings, and trick devices. Nevertheless, it was not easily stageable precisely because of these same qualities, and only in 1930, when Romains had become a well-known, financially successful playwright, did he get an opportunity to write a stage version, put on at the new Théâtre Pigalle with its revolving stage and other complicated machinery. This was more simply entitled *Donogoo,* but, with minor changes in emphasis, it follows the film script fairly closely, and since it antedates the later plays, it is best treated now.

The central idea is simple: that myth, once firmly enough established, can create its own reality. The vehicle of this theme is more complex. Lamendin, one of the seven *copains*, is contemplating suicide on a bridge in Paris when he providentially meets Bénin, who refers him to a quack psychologist, Miguel Rufisque. Rufisque, in his turn, gives Lamendin farcical directions to speak to the first man he meets outside the Paris mosque. This turns out to be Le Trouhadec, Professor of Geography at the Collège de France, who has problems of his own: he is a candidate for election to the Institut de France, but has made an unfortunate blunder in a textbook years before, describing a city of Donogoo-Tonka in South America, whereas in reality no such place existed. Lamendin, his own troubles forgotten, offers to help by establishing a real Donogoo-Tonka where it is supposed to be, and sets about a vast campaign of dishonest publicity, with the help of a crooked banker, to obtain funds and potential settlers. Such is the power of publicity in the present century that in a short time gold-hungry pioneers are pouring into Brazil in search of the mythical city where they hope to strike it rich. Finding nothing and exhausted to the point of collapse, two small expeditions combine and call their joint camp Donogoo-Tonka. Traces of gold are actually found in a nearby stream, further pioneers turn up, and in no time at all Donogoo becomes a thriving settlement, so much so that Lamendin, who has set sail from France dejectedly, fearing that his deception is bound to be unmasked, discovers on his arrival a prosperous city far beyond his dreams. Nor, on his arrival, are the inhabitants eager to give up control to a newcomer to whom in practice they owe nothing, but Lamendin outwits them. Since he is the official chief of the company floated to exploit Donogoo's mineral riches, all he need do is set up camp a few miles away, and establish his own Donogoo-Tonka there, which would rapidly eliminate the existing town. Faced with this threat, the inhabitants yield, and the play ends with Lamendin celebrating his victory with others of the *copains*. Donogoo is now completely under his control, halfway between a patriarchal society and dictatorship. He has even instituted an official religion of Scientific Error, symbolized by a pregnant woman, whose statue with that of Le Trouhadec dominates the town.

Unanimist elements are again obvious. As in *Cromedeyre* or *Le Bourg*, the group is represented by a place and Donogoo is the creation of the animator. But the animator is rapidly becoming transformed into a confidence trickster, although his activities ultimately prove beneficial. Indeed, the play is, in part, a satire on modern advertising techniques: Romains has himself described it as "a heroic comic epic of modern publicity,"[11] but at the same time he insists on joy as the most important note in the play, since only this can enable us to outface the stupidity and ugliness of modern life. If the play is to be taken as a satire, its effect is strangely blurred: no criticism is attached to Lamendin, who first launches a fraudulent company and later takes unscrupulous advantage of his position to establish a dictatorship, nor to Le Trouhadec who is a fool but equally prepared to allow dishonesty to further his ends, nor to lesser figures such as Rufisque, the charlatan, or the dishonest banker. In reality, the gullible public and the pioneers must be the targets of any satirical intentions. The final part of the play where Lamendin rather heavily draws the moral from events, explaining that from scientific error (Le Trouhadec's original blunder), has now sprung scientific truth (the existence of a flourishing town), is in any case irrelevant to the theme of fraudulent publicity and probably has more to do with Romains's disappointment over the unsuccessful outcome of his theories on extraretinal vision. The play is indeed essentially a farce, with humor arising as much from irony of situation as from character. There is no dramatic necessity for the introduction of Rufisque, or for that matter for the play to use characters from *Les Copains* at all. Rufisque anticipates Knock, but is an implausible slapstick figure beside him; Le Trouhadec, the pedantic and essentially stupid, though successful, representative of academic science, is a more significant invention who will become the protagonist of two later comedies, but even he plays no more than an incidental role in triggering off the main events. Pruning the initial scenes with Lamendin's projected suicide, equally irrelevant, and the ponderous didactic conclusion would improve the play's impact. Nevertheless, if initially written for the screen, *Donogoo* marks a further successful step in Romains's artistic development in transferring the comic spirit of *Les Copains* to the medium of drama.

IV *Comedies*

Romains's next comedy, *M. Le Trouhadec saisi par la Débauche*, was produced in May, 1923. Here he takes up again Le Trouhadec, now successfully elected to the Institut, and staying at Monte Carlo under the assumed name of Pessemesse, in pursuit of an actress, Mlle Rolande. An involved plot shows us Le Trouhadec, under Bénin's guidance, winning a fortune in the casino, most of which falls into Rolande's rapacious grasp while the rest is lost in further gambling, after which Le Trouhadec is presented by Trestaillon, an allegedly retired burglar, with a box full of jewels too hot to handle. Bénin saves the situation by obtaining Le Trouhadec's consent to lend his name to a gambling manual ghosted by Josselin, a casino shark. The play, in a highly stylized production by Louis Jouvet—the beginning of a most fruitful theatrical cooperation— was successful, and was taken up by the *Comédie Francaise* in 1955. Notwithstanding, it strikes one today as essentially trivial, weighed down with incredible coincidences, stilted dialogue, and artificial situations. Above all, Le Trouhadec seems too empty a figure to hold one's attention; although Romains has claimed that it was his intention to show how a complete nonentity may be raised by society to a position of importance, this does not alter the fact that the professor is a *fantoche*, a complete caricature who cannot really be taken seriously. Nor is it society which has produced his celebrity, it is two individuals, Lamendin in *Donogoo* and now Bénin, and they are no more than a further development of the animator. At the same time, Unanimism is largely absent from the play, which is basically a comedy of manners treated as farce. We may perhaps conjecture that Unanimist theories were becoming something of an artistic straitjacket. Certainly, from the early 1920's, although there are still many Unanimist traits in his work— his next play *Knock* is largely inspired by it—he tends to use group scenes and descriptions as simply one more of the various literary techniques at his disposal. Nor should we be surprised at this, since it is the fate of all artistic innovations, however revolutionary or all-embracing they may initially have appeared.

M. Le Trouhadec saisi par la Débauche was to prove the occasion for a celebrated literary quarrel. Maurice Boissard (Paul Léautaud), the theater critic who had recently begun reviewing plays for the *N.R.F.*, did not like the play, although he had greatly admired the *beauté sombre et sauvage* of *Cromedeyre*. His review was therefore sharply critical, especially of the play's lack of fantasy, natural-ness, and spontaneity and, referring sarcastically to Romains's Vieux-Colombier lectures on poetic technique, suggested that a better theme would have been a Professor of Poetry surrounded by his pupils (a remark which has its appeal).[12] Romains, always sensitive to criticism, was shown this review before publication, and objected violently. Jacques Rivière, the editor of the *N.R.F.*, felt obliged to side with Romains, since the *N.R.F.* was also publishing Romains's books at the time, and suppressed the offending pages. Léautaud thereupon resigned his post. The incident reflects of course not so much on Romains as on the much-vaunted integrity of the *N.R.F.*; in the outcome, Léautaud was offered the post of theater critic in the weekly *Nouvelles Littéraires* (where he began by printing the review in question), and became something of a celebrity towards the end of his life in the 1950's. Romains, giving his version of the incident recently, adds another gloss by hinting that Léautaud, when secretary of the *Mercure de France* review, was in the habit of "losing" authors' manuscripts, which would at a later date mysteriously turn up in auction sales . . . [13]

Knock was to prove Romains's greatest theatrical success, and indeed one of the best-known plays of the century. Hundreds of thousands of spectators all over the world have laughed at the exploits of Dr. Knock on stage or screen, while perhaps even more significantly, generations of students obliged to pore over the text have actually done so with enjoyment. In *Knock,* Romains breaks away from the *copains* and M. Le Trouhadec, taking instead as his theme the operations of a determined and ruthless medical prac-titioner in transforming an unpromising rural practice into a gold-mine of paying clients. The play consists of three acts only; in the first, we see Knock about to take over the practice of Saint-Meurice—its location unspecified, but a small town in the mountains of South-Central France—and realizing that his predecessor, Dr. Parpalaid, has tricked him about its value. The inhabitants seldom fall ill and even then rarely consult the doctor. Knock sizes up the situation immediately, telling Parpalaid that there is nothing wrong with the practice: it is Parpalaid's own skill which is at fault. Act II contains the meat of the play—Knock in action. He enlists the town crier to announce free treatment every Monday morning, persuades the schoolteacher to give lessons on hygiene, and convinces the pharmacist of the value of close cooperation. Then we pass to the free consultations, where Knock treats two middle-aged women—his first questions devised to discover how prosperous they are—by sending them to bed and insisting on daily visits. All this seems effortlessly easy. His next patients are a couple of village louts who have come for a joke, which turns rapidly against them, as Knock predicts a speedy and gruesome death from alcoholism. The act ends with Knock's mastery complete. In the final act, we move forward three months, when Parpalaid returns for his first quarterly payment. The whole town has been transformed; its only hotel is now a clinic, and with 250 patients to visit in their homes, Knock has hardly a minute to himself. Needless to say, the takings are rolling in; while his information about the prosperity of the district is so good that, against the seventeen households which the tax collector believes have an annual income of over twelve thousand francs, Knock counts 1,502. Parpalaid, at first incredulous, let alone suspicious, falls so much under Knock's sway that when the play ends he too is convinced he is seriously ill.

Knock was put on in December, 1923, by Louis Jouvet who, strangely enough, was anxious about the public's reactions to the play, which he thought cut too near the bone (André Pascal's play *Le Caducée* had had to be withdrawn in 1911 due to organized medical opposition).[14] In fact it seems likely that some of the play's success was due to Jouvet's production with its meticulous timing and gesture, while his portrayal of the title role was one of the classic performances of the age. His faith in the play was richly rewarded since revivals of it kept his troupe afloat for years through many a crisis, while it made Romains a wealthy man. *Knock*, like his other successful comedies, is basically a farce, and may be seen as a lineal descendant of his student *canulars*. The hero is a further stage in the animator, and the main theme is really the power of suggestion; its application to the field of medicine is subsidiary, though in showing doctors—Parpalaid no less than Knock, although the former is incompetent—as viewing their profession primarily from the aspect of material gain, Romains was reverting to the satirical strain running from the Middle Ages to its apogee in Molière's *Malade Imaginaire*. In this he turns sharply away from another tradition, that of Balzac, Flaubert, and Zola, where the doctor becomes a protagonist of positive scientific progress, fighting suffering and ignorance. Ignorance is precisely the material on which Knock works; he is able to blind the inhabitants of Saint-Meurice with science, an essential part of the publicity campaign which is what his efforts amount to.

Looked at dispassionately, the implications of *Knock* are serious, and critics have talked of Romains's methods as leading to political dictatorship if applied in that sphere. Ironically, the play was banned in Germany under the Nazis. As in *Donogoo*, the satirical aspects tell most heavily against the dupes—*malades imaginaires*—rather than against the wily doctor. But we should not forget that *Knock* is a play written for the stage, not a documentary based on actual observation. Many of its effects, above all the entire situation in Act III, are based on gross exaggeration and are not really plausible. This does not prevent it from being genuinely funny, and this is the greatest quality of the play: it makes people laugh. Comedy of character is combined with comedy of situation, comedy of language—the extremely witty *répliques*—and with comedy of gesture on stage, to form one of the most amusing and dramatically effective plays of our age.

During rehearsals, Jouvet had decided that *Knock* was too short a play to provide a full evening's theatergoing and Romains therefore wrote a one-act play to accompany it, *Amédée et les Messieurs en rang*.[15] Completed in four days, *Amédée* is subtitled *mystère en un acte*, although *fantaisie* might be a better description. The central idea is how Unanimist life is breathed into an institution, one of the shoeshine saloons which are a feature of Barcelona, recently visited by Romains. Amédée, an employee, suddenly leaves a client with one shoe dirty, and refuses to return to work. The *patron* and the other employee go to look for him, and conversation among the clients reveals that the woman Amédée loves has been taken from him by the man whose shoes he is shining. Gradually the other six customers become a Unanimist group, and go out to inspect the lady in question. Amédée returns, but his humiliation is complete, since everyone now knows the truth. The play ends with Amédée reconciled to his situation through his pride in his skill, and the saloon about to be transformed into a private shoeshine club where he can display the finest techniques of his art. Jouvet was enthusiastic about *Amédée*, but the play left the audience cold; it was in any case completely outshone by *Knock*, and its somewhat bitter tone contrasts oddly with the full-blooded gaiety of the other play. The dialogue, too, especially Amédée's lines, sounds artificial and "literary," while the Unanimist plot is a little strained. Not too much should be expected of one-act plays, but nevertheless *Amédée* remains unsubstantial.

In 1924, Romains wrote another one-act play to replace *Amédée* in a revival of *Knock*. This was *La Scintillante*, now using the central idea of a small-town bicycle shop. "La Scintillante" is the name of the shop, though it also fits the attractive widow who runs it and whose charms attract aspirants into her premises, among them Vicomte Calixte de Percepieu, the son of the local landowner. It turns out that Calixte is less attracted by the lady than by business and the possibility of working there; he finally even brings his grumpy father round to forget his social position and to take an interest in the shop, which might be developed into a motorcycle or automobile manufacture. Again, apart from the novelty of a bicycle shop on stage, this play seems extremely slight. The dialogue is stylized to the point of being stilted, as in many of Romains's comedies. This is acceptable in *Knock*, with his intention of impressing the ignorant, but less so here where it merely sounds implausible and artificial. The play again illustrates Romains's interest in modern means of transport: trains, cars, bicycles; but with an indeterminate ending, the play fails to grip one's interest.

In Romains's next comedy, *Le Mariage de Le Trouhadec*, we return to his earlier hero. By now, the geographer is a national figure, and an unscrupulous journalist, Mirouette, invites him to lend his name to a new political party, the *Comité des Honnêtes Gens*. This requires that he break with his mistress, Rolande, and most of the involved plot deals with her maneuvering and with the proposal that Le Trouhadec should marry Geneviève, daughter of Baronne Gentil-Durand, the question hingeing on whether Le Trouhadec is still sexually potent. Meanwhile, the *Comité*, trained by Bénin to act as one man, gets completely out of hand and becomes a kind of inquisition to root out the dishonest from around them. In the end, Le Trouhadec, with Bénin's aid, succeeds in disentangling himself from Rolande, and regains control over the *Comité*, so that the play can end with his marriage in close prospect. Performed, again by Jouvet, in January, 1925, the play proved a failure. This time Jouvet's stylization did not attract the audience, and it is not difficult to see why. Humor has given way to satire, but the objects of the satire—Mirouette, the Baronne, only too keen to marry her daughter off even to an impotent old man, the *Comité*—all lack substance. We are left with a clumsy and heavy play, in doubtful taste, a great contrast to the brilliant simplicity of *Knock*. No doubt Romains on reflection realized this, and at this point permanently abandoned the *copains* and the geographer.

With *Démétrios*, produced the same year,[16] the animator has become simply a barefaced rogue in the time-hallowed tradition of the stage swindler. In this one-act sketch, we see Démétrios presenting himself at the household of M. Gallargues and, by smooth talk, first persuading M. Gallargues to invest a large sum of money in a dubious speculation, then conquering the heart of Mme Léa, Gallargues's widowed but still appetizing daughter, all this despite his admission that he is a criminal wanted by police in several parts of the world. Jouvet's portrayal of Démétrios emphasized his flashy villainy, and all in all the play is simply a repeat of *Knock* on a much inferior level.

V *Later Drama*

Romains's next play, *Le Dictateur*, produced in 1926, is very different. Here he chooses a political theme: how a revolutionary leader can, once in office and under the pressure of events, suspend constitutional rights and take absolute power into his own hands. At the start of the play, Denis has succeeded in bringing about the parliamentary defeat of the existing government. According to constitutional convention, the king ought therefore to call on him to form the next government, as the architect of the downfall of the preceding one; despite doubts about the wisdom of bringing a revolutionary to power, the king nevertheless does so, on the theory that the responsibilities of office will tame Denis. On his side, Denis too has qualms, and he is passionately advised against acceptance by Féréol, a friend since childhood and another revolutionary who has avoided all compromise with the existing régime by refusing election to Parliament. Denis accepts, and finds the king much more human and responsible than expected. He now begins to feel obligations not merely towards the toiling masses, but towards society as a whole. Féréol on his side foments a general strike, against which Denis feels obliged to take strong measures. He summons Féréol and tries to explain his motives, but, in a bitter quarrel, Féréol angrily refuses to accept them, while Denis sees no alternative to arresting his former friend. At the end of the play he possesses virtually absolute political power.

The starting point of the play is Briand's action in suppressing the threatened 1910 general strike by measures including mobilizing striking railwaymen as army reservists, and his subsequent declaration that he was prepared to use even illegal methods to preserve order; the episode is extensively treated in Volume IX of *Les Hommes de Bonne Volonté*. Greatly impressed by Briand's determination, Romains had begun a first, verse, draft of *Le Dictateur* in 1910–1912, but had abandoned it. By 1926 he had an even more relevant model of dictator, Mussolini, who, it is easy to forget, was widely admired at that time for his determination in seizing power to suppress anarchy and strikes in Italy in 1922. But *Le Dictateur* is not a *pièce à clef*; and Romains probably made its setting a monarchy less in imitation of contemporary Italy than to prevent close identification with the political situation in France. The character of the king, if not the queen as well, is also needed for purely dramatic purposes, to show Denis's political evolution.

Romains wished *Le Dictateur* to be staged at the Comédie Française, since he considered that only there, with its experienced classically-trained actors, could full justice be done to his serious theme, but after difficulties because the Comédie found it politically too strong meat, it was produced by Jouvet. Romains was probably right, since the play was only a partial success in France, though translations were outstandingly successful, perhaps ominously so, in Berlin, Vienna, and Budapest. Looked at today, *Le Dictateur* suffers from the fault of most works on a political theme: it has been overtaken by events. Above all, the theory that revolutionary leaders will be restrained by the exercise of power was calamitously tested in Germany in 1933. There is an air of unreality about the play, as there is about Shaw's *Apple Cart*, probably because Romains has introduced an imaginary monarchy, with the king and queen on stage. Moreover, Act I, with almost farcical secret policemen, is out of tone with the rest of the play and unnecessary for exposition purposes. The political issues are oversimplified, and for an experienced politician, Denis at times appears naïve. The best scenes in the play are the confrontations between Denis and Féréol, with Denis's realization that his aims and ideals are entirely different from those of his closest friend; and there is no doubt that his growing belief in order is put forward as the desirable ideal rather than Féréol's sanguinary faith in violent revolution at any cost. At this point, Romains clearly saw dictators as a valuable bulwark against revolution and anarchy; he was not alone in this, but in the next decade had to revise his views radically.

Unanimism is virtually absent from *Le Dictateur*: the theme of friendship treated in Denis's relationship with Féréol and with the king, who on becoming king had to break with the only friend of his youth, is much broader. Perhaps our conclusion should be that the theater is not the best vehicle for treatment of complex political issues, which were now coming to occupy more and more of Romains's attention. This is borne out by the political essays which he began to write in the late 1920's, and in many volumes of *Les Hommes de Bonne Volonté*, where he was able both to delve into these topics more deeply, and to relate them to the actual political history of his own country.

In *Jean le Maufranc* we have the theme of the *homme traqué*, the individual harassed by the demands of modern society. We have come a long way from the joyful merging of the individual in the group, whether or not Romains was using his own experiences in the play. Once again the theme has a respectable literary ancestry; no less than Molière's *Misanthrope*. Jean's problems are to be taken as representative of those facing contemporary man: he is searched by customs officials, has to endure inquisitions from his wife and from the income tax authorities, and above all feels that freedom is a deceptive illusion. He discovers a body calling itself the *International League for the Protection of Modern Man*, composed of a bishop, doctors and other worthies, but investigation shows the League is no more than a collection of interfering busybodies, who would force mankind to be free by measures including compulsory identity cards, organized Sunday recreation, and a ban not only on alcohol, but also on tea, coffee, and tobacco! Jean therefore decides on hypocrisy as the only method of preserving his shrinking liberty, arranges a fraudulent bankruptcy, and takes refuge with Pierrette, a young girl unaware of his identity. The play ends on an indeterminate note after Jean has confessed his dishonest behavior to the bishop, but is unable to accept the solace of the Christian God. His need is for some other religion to fill the void.

The best part of the play is undoubtedly the satire of the League, yet this is mainly presented in the second of the five acts, which results in a lack of unity and weakening of dramatic interest. The 1926 production by Georges Pitoëff, since the scene-changes were beyond the capabilities of Jouvet's small stage, was not to the public taste. Romains recast the play, which was put on again in 1930 under the title of *Musse ou l'École de l'Hypocrisie*, and was this time well received. Its dramatic impact had been made firmer, notably by omitting the idyll with Pierrette, and the activities of the League are given more prominence, as is the bitter attack on the tyranny of the modern state. We seem to be at the opposite pole from the ideas of *Le Dictateur*; however, this contradiction need not surprise us. Even Ibsen in *The Wild Duck* appears to contradict entirely the ideas of his preceding play, *The Pillars of Society*, which in no way detracts from the dramatic merits of either one. In Romains's case, despite the shrill, almost hysterical note (tax-avoidance is a time-honored sport in France, but it scarcely seems iniquitous simply to levy income tax), he found a theme which struck an echo in his audience, and one which has maintained its relevance in succeeding decades.

Volpone is the product of a collaboration. Stefan Zweig had made a lively German adaptation of Ben Jonson's comedy of the old miser stripped of his wealth by his own servant, and Romains now made a French version of Zweig's play. *Volpone* was successfully produced by Charles Dullin in 1928 and has since been revived several times.

Romains's last single-act play was *Le Déjeuner marocain* (1929). Credulity once again provides the dramatic mainspring, with another plausible rogue, Mercus, acting as middleman between a Moroccan princeling, Moulay M'rassine, who wishes to add a French girl to his existing collection of wives, and M. and Mme Tastignac, whose daughter Liane is to form the basis of the transaction. Since Moulay is to pay a bride price of two hundred thousand francs, the Tastignacs would therefore avoid paying a dowry and would instead be enriched. Liane, far from being an unfortunate and unwilling victim of her parents' cupidity, accepts the situation with hardheaded lucidity and makes Moulay agree to follow the *coutume de Libourne*—a small French town near Bordeaux from which the Tastignacs hail, and which Mercus has managed to convince Moulay is one of the finest cities in France. The play ends with all parties satisfied and with Mercus, as he pockets his commission, asking the Tastignacs if they have any more daughters. Again there is little trace of Unanimism; credulity as a theme is nothing new, and the play in some ways recalls a *turquerie* such as *Le Bourgeois Gentilhomme*. The prevailing tone is that of farce, since none of the characters is really credible, nor is the action, interspersed with facile slapstick such as belching at a banquet. The play is thus too unrealistic to be a genuine satire on either Arab gullibility or bourgeois French rapacity and hypocrisy. In general, *Le Déjeuner* is somewhat slight, and uses a stereotyped view of "exotic" Arab customs, in a way which has since become unacceptable.

Boën ou la Possession des Biens was staged in 1930, although there are hints that its composition goes back to 1926. Its theme is the effect of wealth on modern man. Boën, owner of a small factory making mechanical products, decides to find out exactly what his financial state is. To his surprise, he discovers he has a fortune of two million francs, and receives a further windfall when a rich American, Parker, buys from him the rights to an invention, the Stolix, for an additional five million. Faced with this unexpected wealth, Boën feels twinges of guilt because his engineer, Hébingre, is the real inventor of the Stolix, though he has made over his patent. But Boën's attempts to divest himself of some of his wealth to those around him come to naught, since all, for various reasons, refuse. Romains evidently intended some broad significance, since the American Parker, with his idea of never leaving money idle and constantly producing more and more wealth, is contrasted with Boën's secretary, Sabine, recently returned from the Soviet Union from where she has brought back a completely different set of values: comradeship in the common struggle to improve material conditions, free from the millstone of individual riches. However, these two extremes are too crudely presented, and the total dramatic effect of the play remains confused. *Boën* proved a failure, perhaps partly because Romains had three other successes running at the same time, *Donogoo*, *Musse*, and a revival of *Knock*. In comparison, *Boën* appeared pale and abstruse. Possibly a tightened-up revision, in the manner of *Musse*, might have succeeded; but the theme of money has consistently, since *L'Avare*, proved difficult and dangerous for box office success.

With his three-act comedy, *Le Roi masqué* (1931), Romains created a gay fantasy, showing a very different treatment of matters of state from *Le Dictateur*. The king of a Central European Ruritania, weary of his ill-tempered wife and the intrigues of his Chancellor's supporters, who are, incidentally, homosexuals, decides to stay incognito in Paris under the cover of testing a new submarine at a secret naval base. His first experiences in Paris are hardly promising: his interpreter Piéchèvre introduces him to an actress, Sourval, yet the king as an ordinary person is of much less interest to her than Piéchèvre himself. He visits the studio of the painter Abrabanel, who attacks his contemporaries such as Picasso and Matisse, but proves a charlatan himself. Meanwhile Piéchèvre has squandered nearly all the royal purse. The king's luck changes when he meets Marcelle, a young salesgirl who loves him for himself, without, of course, remotely realizing his true identity. Affairs of state force the king to return home, since he is faced with a threatened *coup d'état* by the queen and Chancellor. Telling Marcelle the truth about himself, he takes her with him disguised as a sailor, but the two are discovered together by the queen, who thinks Marcelle is a boy. The Chancellor is delighted and reconciled by the king's apparent homosexuality, which the queen too accepts, so the play can end happily. Yet the king, to conceal his true relations with Marcelle, will have to continue a life of deceit.

The prevailing tone of the play is farcical, and Romains flails out wildly, but wittily, in all directions, mocking equally all his characters except the king and Marcelle. In essence, *Le Roi masqué* is lighthearted *boulevard* theater, at the opposite pole to the immense ambitions of his early verse drama; and with this play he deserted the theater for some years, thus closing a busy chapter in his artistic career.

VI   *The* Psyché *Trilogy*

In 1922 had appeared *Lucienne*, the first volume in a new venture by Romains. His theme is, quite simply, ideal love: the celebration of the couple which we have already seen as a Unanimist *dieu* in the *Prières*. Now, in Romains's first extended venture into the novel, he is able to treat the subject at greater length. We know some details of the genesis of the trilogy;[17] the basic idea, Romains states, goes back, like most of his major subjects, to 1907–1911, but he did not start writing until 1920. Originally, only one volume was planned, but he rapidly realized that his material would require more development. Nevertheless, *Lucienne* appeared by itself as an independent novel, and its sequels, *Le Dieu des corps* and *Quand le navire . . .* did not appear until 1928 and 1929. Romains's pre-occupation with the theater in the mid-1920's no doubt explains the considerable delay.

The title of the trilogy, *Psyché*, was not settled until the appearance of the second volume, as the result of the publisher's urgings, since the individual volumes would be likely to sell better under a common title. We should not, therefore, expect the novel to be an explicit contemporary treatment of the Psyche myth. In fact, the first volume shows the origin and development of the ideal relationship between Lucienne and Pierre Febvre; the second treats their marriage and the development of physical love, again in ideal terms; while the third and last attempts to illustrate how even physical separation can be overcome by extraordinary sensibility and exercise of will, thus making the Unanimist couple virtually indestructible. *Lucienne* is narrated in the first person by the heroine, a girl who after her mother's remarriage has decided to leave Paris and to earn her own living from piano lessons in D***, a provincial town where she has an old friend, a teacher at the girls' lycée. In the early months, Lucienne finds it difficult to make ends meet, but eventually arranges well-paid lessons with a family named Barbelenet. M. Barbelenet is the director of the local railroad workshops, D*** being an important junction, and the family lives in a strange house entirely surrounded by glittering steel tracks. Lucienne teaches the Barbelenet daughters, and meets Pierre, a ship's purser convalescent at a nearby spa and a distant cousin frequently invited by Mme Barbelenet with matrimonial intentions. Nothing is further from Pierre's mind, but he and Lucienne im-mediately fall in love, not so much by a *coup de foudre* but with tranquil confidence, and the volume ends with their engagement. The action is indeed somewhat slim, and noticeably lacking in the exuberance of Romains's earlier fiction: necessarily so perhaps, given the modest and unassuming personality of Lucienne. Romains draws on autobiographical elements: D*** is based on Laon, where he had been particularly impressed by a house similar to the Barbelenets' and his treatment of this house, an island in a sea of steel rails, is the clearest point of contact between the novel and his earlier enthusiasm for modern industrial society. Lucienne herself is at least partly an idealized version of Gabrielle, not so much in physical description since Romains throughout the trilogy concentrates more on the psychological, but in her sensitive love for music. But at the same time, she exists in her own fictional right, just as Pierre must not be confused with Romains himself. Intelligent, cultured, independent-minded, yet loyal, virtuous, chaste, and above all, intensely sensitive, Lucienne evidently represents Romains's ideal marriage partner; however, like most idealized figures, somewhat lacks credibility and therefore interest.

In *Le Dieu des Corps*, Romains switches the first person narrative to Pierre, who is thus able to recount from his own viewpoint his meeting with Lucienne and their engagement. He is shown as an intelligent well-educated man, with a keen interest in scientific problems, more analytical and less sensitive than Lucienne, but sharing with her a highly developed self-awareness. Over a third of *Le Dieu des Corps* is devoted to this initial exposé, followed by the central section, an extended treatment in careful, sober language, of the physical sexual relationship on their wedding night, given with what were for the time unusually frank and precise details. It is this that gained the book considerable notoriety, especially in the English translation, *The Body's Rapture*, still to be found in the restricted section of certain libraries. But to consider the book pornographic is to misunderstand Romains's purpose entirely. In his intellectual analysis of a sexual relationship based on completely free choice, mutual confidence and respect, his aim is to show the attainment of spiritual unity through the physical, a kind of religion of the flesh in which Lucienne and Pierre are at the same time initiates and celebrants. This is clearly shown both in the wedding night episode and the final hundred pages which cover the few weeks between the marriage and Pierre's return to active duty on his ship. More and more the factual description of the physical side of marriage for love merges into the problem of physical separation.

This is the theme of the final volume, *Quand le navire . . . .* Here Romains explicitly develops the hints of supernatural powers which have been made in works such as *Le Vin blanc de La Villette*.

Lucienne, who has earlier visited Pierre's ship and knows its internal geography, by sheer effort of will manages to "project" herself into Pierre's cabin one evening, so powerfully that not only does her spiritual presence enter Pierre's consciousness, but her corporeal presence is attested after she has left by the imprint of her body where she has sat on Pierre's bunk. This is indeed a strange theme and Romains seems uncomfortable in handling it. Nominally, Pierre is again the narrator, but as certain events have to be shown from Lucienne's side, she is deemed to keep lengthy journals, to which he later has access. The result is a certain clumsiness and artificiality. Nor is this supernatural—Romains might prefer to call it suprarational—event alone in the book: a passenger called Podomiecki is introduced who also illustrates indubitable powers of clairvoyance. No doubt intended to bolster the supernatural theme, Podomiecki merely complicates it and increases the reader's uneasiness. Moreover, the main theme is not exhaustively handled. There are hints that this first self-projection by Lucienne will be followed by others where her "presence" in Pierre's cabin will be taken to the point of physical possession; yet nothing comes of this—the technical difficulties of narrating (convincingly) such a telepathic union would obviously be formidable. Romains ends the novel in a curiously indeterminate way, with Pierre suddenly jumping forward many years into the future—the main action antedates the 1914–1918 War—to state that the "frontier" was broken only once, and now Lucienne and he lead the life of countless ordinary couples, since he holds a shore job and physical separation is no longer a problem. It is almost as if Romains had wearied of his own novel, which may indeed be the case, since by 1929 his marital life had become far from ideal and the frame of mind in which he had conceived the theme of the couple evidently lay far behind him.

Viewed in retrospect, the *Psyché* trilogy is obviously overshadowed by the enormous novel which was to follow it. At the time, nevertheless, it attained considerable success. *Lucienne* almost gained the Goncourt Prize for 1922, being narrowly defeated by Henri Béraud's *Le Martyre de l'obèse*, a novel which has signally failed to survive. (The success of Béraud, a virulently Right-wing writer later condemned to death, until reprieved, for collaboration in World War II, did not prevent him from publishing violent diatribes against Romains, all the more galling as Romains was linked in them with Gide, for whose work Romains's admiration was far from unbounded, and whose moral influence, especially as regards homosexuality, he profoundly deplored.) Certainly it marks an attempt by Romains to establish himself in a new literary field, and in this he succeeded. New for him, since, seen in the light of the French novel as a whole, the trilogy appears less a Unanimist work than a return to the central stream of the *roman personnel*, the novel of psychological analysis. There is nothing new, after all, in the assertion that the married couple is one flesh, and the very idealism, the search for purity even in the most physical of embraces, again recalls the idealizing tendencies of the *roman personnel*. Where *Psyché* is most original is of course in its final volume with the theme of telepathic self-projection. This in part is a transposition of extraretinal vision: Lucienne, sitting in her Marseilles apartment, "sees" Pierre's ship, its corridors, and his cabin in terms very close to those used by Romains in his book on eyeless sight. At the same time, this mystical power of the couple is directly connected with the Unanimist idea of the psychic continuum. This again illustrates the irrational basis of much of Unanimism: any psychological backing would have to depend on fairly crude dichotomy between mind and body, by means of which the mind, under the dynamic of a dominating will, could somehow "transfer" the body along the psychical continuum to rejoin the other half of the couple. That these and similar questions continued to fascinate Romains is shown by frequent indications in *Les Hommes de Bonne Volonté*, while virtually the same themes will form the subject of *Violation de frontières* twenty years later.

Yet the third volume is at the same time the least satisfactory. The supernatural has obsessed writers for centuries, illustrating perhaps a difference in temperament between the artist and the scientist; but its most successful use in literature has undoubtedly been to create horror. The "Gothic" novel has recently been returning to favor, while its derivative, the ghost story, has never lost it. To utilize the supernatural in an effectively positive way is much more difficult: Romains's theories can be illustrated but remain undemonstrable, and as a consequence, largely implausible. In the ghost story, the reader wants in any case nothing better than to be frightened, but in *Quand le navire . . .*, any similar "suspension of disbelief" is awkward since the events described do not correspond to the accepted facts of existence, but depend only on the author's fantasy and are not really credible. The theme of separation had in any case, on a much more profound level, been the tragic experience of tens of millions of European couples during the War, in countless cases to prove a separation for eternity. In this context, a couple of weeks spent by Pierre away from his wife, but in conditions of considerable luxury on an ocean liner, pale into triviality. This adds to a general impression of thinness of texture throughout, of overcerebral abstraction: a lack of the density of *Les Hommes de Bonne Volonté*; at some point a comparative judgment becomes inevitable, and the Naturalist tradition Romains was next to adopt allowed him greater elbow room without any sacrifice of intensity.

Perhaps *Psyché* could have been compressed into one volume after all; certain episodes appear drawn out beyond necessity, such as the description of the Barbelenet family and their strange house. Humanity being what it is, an account of a sexual relationship in terms of immediate, complete, and permanent harmony, inevitably sounds too good to be true—or to be interesting. Romains's treatment in any event strikes us as overidealized and abstract, while there is occasional indulgence in excessive sentimentality. The first person narration, first by Lucienne and then by Pierre, offers too little variation. This form of narrative is especially suitable for introspective analysis, where the single viewpoint is essential; it is less effective in narrating action, since this has to be presented entirely in the past, sharply reducing dramatic possibilities. It enabled Romains to experiment with new techniques, such as the interior monologue, specifically a fully conscious, not unconscious, monologue, while the reflections of Pierre in particular allow treatment of some interesting abstract psychological problems. But it is frequently only too obvious that it is Romains himself writing or thinking and not the nominal protagonist. Above all, the trilogy lacks the self-confidence of Romains's best work. It is as if he did not quite know where he was going, and in the later volumes he was clearly not following a detailed earlier plan since he incorporates a large slab of not very relevant description of New York, only visited two years after the publication of *Lucienne*. We may suspect also that he had Freud looking over one shoulder, and Proust over the other, unable to accept completely the implications of their work and yet equally unable to ignore it and therefore forced to attempt to reach what he himself hoped would be a new depth in the field of sexual and psychological relationships.

VII   Chants des Dix Années

Romains continued to write poetry during the 1920's, and after individual publication, the separate works were collected as *Chants des Dix Années* in 1928. *Amour Couleur de Paris*, a poem of some fifty lines, appeared as a *plaquette* in 1921; in it, the poet celebrates his love for his wife, and his feeling for Paris. Each of the five short sections ends with the mysteriously haunting refrain of the poem's title. The tone is one of quiet lyricism, much more musical than most of Romains's work, recalling even Verlaine:

> *Tout le meilleur de l'azur,*
> *N'en reste-t-il qu'une cendre—*
> *Soir impalpable—*
> > *et des murs?*

> *Pourtant les vitres encore*
> *Te font des sources de ciel,*
> *Tremblantes, mais non taries;*

> *Du ciel pour une heure encore,*

> *Du bleu qui serre le cœur,*

> *Amour couleur de Paris.*[18]

Given its brevity, the poem cannot be considered a major work, but in it Romains communicates a sense of harmony and repose after the thirst for action and movement of his prewar poetry, and the anguish of *Europe*. Published with *Amour Couleur de Paris* were two further poems, *Palais du monde* and *Ode*. The theme of the first is the threatening storm despite the blue skies, and of the second, the poet's deep discouragement faced with the enormous task of repairing the *affreuse blessure* of the War.

Ode Génoise, published in 1925, follows naturally on *Europe* and was written in 1923–1924 after a brief stay in Genoa.[19] The theme is once more the war, and Romains's technique is again to contrast the stupidity of useless bloodshed with the simple joys of peacetime Europe. As the poet sits in a wine shop in the Italian seaport, his memories take him back to other scenes, such as a visit to the Rhône glacier in Switzerland, or a crowd dancing the *sardana* in the streets of Barcelona. But he cannot help also remembering the War, which has solved nothing:

> *Je ne puis pas oublier la misère de ce temps*[20]

which acts as a refrain in a long section where he makes skillful use of the fourteen-syllable line. In his pessimism, the poet even wonders if prehistoric man was not more fortunate than his twentieth-century descendant:

> *Dans la forêt scythique et les joncs de l'Elbe*
> *Des hommes velus rampaient mieux réfugiés que nous.*[21]

The poem is weaker when Romains rather self-consciously takes on the role of spokesman for ordinary humble people against politicians, and we detect a certain note of false humility here:

> *Je suis né de petites gens*
> *Gagnant peu pour beaucoup de peine,*
> *Mes aïeux ont tiré de terre*
> *Plus de blé qu'ils n'ont eu de pain.*[22]

The War, unfortunately, was not so simple, not merely a conspiracy by *les puissants de ce monde*. In all the belligerent countries, war fever swept through the population without distinction of class in the initial stages, and Romains simply detracts from the poignancy of his cry by seeking scapegoats. He is on safer ground when he calls up the millions of dead in a dignified but poignant lament:

> *Morts d'Europe, on vous reconnaît;*
> *Tués, c'est vous,*
> *En képi, en casque, en bonnet,*
> *Puant le sang, trempés de pluie,*
> *Mordus de poux.*[23]

As so often in Romains's verse, he is at his best when he avoids abstractions and concentrates on simple emotions and concrete images.

VIII *Essays*

In 1927 Romains published in book form his first collection of essays, *La Vérité en bouteilles*, which date from 1909 to the mid-1920's and deal with his literary attitudes and aims. The earlier ones are polemical and form an apologia for Unanimism and Romains's poetic practice; the later ones, his literary reputation assured, are more mellow and seek to establish the principles of a modern Classicism. Romains wishes to aim at the *juste milieu* between pure imitation of earlier poetic forms on the one hand, and wild innovation on the other. He is dubious about the influence of Romanticism: genius is not enough for literary creation, and some kind of self-discipline is necessary. Nor are Naturalism or Symbolism adequate aesthetics, the former because of its use of the abstract thesis, the latter for its overindulgence in symbols, marking a snobbish, élitist view which prefers the invisible world to the real. However, Romains in no way despises the nineteenth century, and he declares that no century has ever been more suited to prepare a Classical age. The new Classicism will, of course, be on the lines of Unanimism and Romains's own work; he has only contempt for the Dada movement, which he sees as negation and exultation for their own sake, followed inevitably by disillusionment, bitterness, and self-disgust. For the rest of his life, this Neoclassical literary theory will remain Romains's credo.

The second collection of essays, entitled *Problèmes d'aujourd'hui*, followed in 1931. These are a mixed bag, some political, some aesthetic, with a critique of psychoanalysis for good measure. The first section, *Pour que l'Europe soit*, consists of the articles which Romains wrote for an American newspaper in 1915, but which never appeared; however, he believed they had gained an influential private circulation, and even flattered himself that they had helped President Wilson develop his peace proposals. Romains saw himself as a European primarily, not a Frenchman; war was anachronistic, and the only sensible aim for the participants must not be victory or a search for scapegoats, but a just peace leading to European unity. From the vantage point of today, these ideas seem unchallengeable, but add up to little more than good intentions, impotent unless matched by equal good intentions from the other side. In practice, Romains's concrete program for the maintenance of peace, once reestablished, was nebulous. He suggests a reduction in armaments, and an increase in the number of small sovereign states; both were indeed attempted and proved unsuccessful, and the second contradicts the belief that Europe is a whole and the idea of nationality outdated. The second essay deals with the League of Nations, which Romains sees as needing authoritative sanctions, some elective content, representatives responsible to constituents rather than simply nominated by governments. Thus it might develop into a United States of Europe. Here Romains puts his finger on two glaring weaknesses in the League, the first of which was to prove its downfall.

Romains's third essay, on psychoanalysis, dates from 1922. With his usual acuity, he distinguishes four common uses of the term psychoanalysis: investigation of the mind viewed broadly; a theory of development of neuroses; a therapeutic method of treating neuroses; and general psychological theory. Romains accepts Freud's brilliance, which he sees as penetrating further than poetic intuition into the knowledge of the human heart; yet although Freudian theory explains some neuroses, in other cases it fails, and Romains wonders if its therapeutic successes are outweighed by its failures. Again, this is an attitude well ahead of its time: in the early 1920's, Freudianism was just becoming the vogue in France, and attitudes were largely split between enthusiastic acceptance and ferocious rejection. Romains's reasoned recognition of Freud's insights and doubts about their universal applicability represent a common viewpoint today.

The fourth essay consists of the lecture, *Petite introduction à l'Unanimisme*, given in various European countries, already mentioned. The fifth, *Sur l'Art dramatique* (1926), should be read together with Romains's long introduction to Berthold Mahn's sketchbook, *Souvenirs du Vieux-Colombier*, of the same year. In both, Romains—at the height of his career in the theater while his fame as a novelist still lay in the future—claims it is considerably more difficult to write a successful play than a novel. This is because the drama demands density and form, a distillation of the prolix material of the novel, into which almost anything may be integrated without difficulty. For the cultured, educated spectator in the theater is much more exigent than the same man with a novel. This claim is probably true; it is notorious that some of the greatest French novelists rapidly came to grief when they turned their attentions to the theater. Yet behind this argument there stands the Classicist assumption that the drama is the supreme literary form, and verse drama the highest ideal of all. This at any rate is Romains's position in 1926, though he might have modified it later in line with the prefatory claims of *Les Hommes de Bonne Volonté*—itself, ironically enough, a brilliant example of the portmanteau qualities of the novel outlined here.

The final essay is a venture into art criticism: a comparison of the

sculpture of Rodin and Maillol. Romains strikes a fairly conventional contrast between Maillol's equilibrium and harmony, and Rodin's
pathos and movement, one which we may define in terms of form
versus expression. Both are equally valid, but the ideal would be
a synthesis of the two.

CHAPTER 4

Years of Involvement

I *War and Exile*

THE 1930's were for Romains a decade of unparalleled activity. Not only literary, though these years saw the completion of some score volumes of *Les Hommes de Bonne Volonté*, but also semipolitical activity of various kinds. This resulted in further extensive traveling of a more serious nature. After attending the P.E.N. Congress in Budapest in 1932, Romains went to the succeeding one in Dubrovnik the following year, only to find that the German delegates had been replaced by Nazi nominees; he took a leading part in demanding that these be excluded. In 1936 he became International President of the P.E.N. Movement, no prestigious sinecure, given the plight of dozens of refugee writers from Germany and elsewhere. Throughout the decade Romains was busy traveling and lecturing, in London in 1932, at the Institute of International Cooperation at Madrid, under the short-lived Spanish Republic, in Spring, 1933, in Germany and Scandinavia the same year, in Rumania, Poland, Italy, and Germany in 1934, in Portugal as a guest of the government in 1935, and again in London that Fall. In 1936 he revisited the United States, following this up with a cruise to South America. It is well-nigh impossible to disentangle his journeys in the last feverish years preceding the 1939 outbreak of war, but he has said himself that in 1938 he visited fourteen different countries and met six different Heads of State.

Romains's political activity took several forms. In the first place, as we have seen, he was deeply concerned with the suppression of liberty of expression, especially in Nazi Germany. At the same time, the specter of European war continued to haunt him, and he still saw a Franco-German *rapprochement* as the best, indeed the only, means of averting this. The League of Nations was obviously helpless, while Britain could not be counted on to support France in a policy of force towards resurgent Germany. This being so, Romains continued to preach Franco-German understanding, despite his knowledge of Nazi persecutions, as the lesser evil, which explains his acceptance of the humiliating Munich agreement in Fall, 1938, on the grounds that a war postponed may never take place. After the fall of France, he wrote a bitter justification of his actions and ideas in the 1930's, *Sept mystères du destin de l'Europe,* and we shall deal with the question in more detail later. Romains had also become involved, willy-nilly, in internal French politics. After the attempted Right-wing coup d'état of February, 1934, he found himself at the head of the July 9 Movement, a short-lived affair spanning a variety of nominal political allegiances. Some Frenchmen, if not Romains himself, evidently saw the Movement as a means of surmounting factional politics and indeed taking over the government, with Romains as national leader, though it is difficult to see how this could have been done without in the process destroying the democratic and republican values they were claiming to preserve. In any event, the Movement rapidly came to nothing.

The 1930's saw considerable changes in Romains's personal life. His father died in 1933, his mother five years later. We may infer from Jallez's reflections in a similar situation in *Les Hommes de Bonne Volonté,* that Romains profoundly regretted having been unable to devote more time to his parents in their old age. As we have seen, too, his first marriage broke down in the early 1930's, and divorce was followed in December, 1936, by his second marriage, to Lise Dreyfus, whom he had met some years previously and who had more recently acted as his secretary. The honeymoon trip took the couple to tropical Africa.

After the outbreak of war in September, 1939, Romains visited Belgium and Switzerland on government missions; there was no question but to support the French war effort to the utmost. On the invasion of France in June, 1940, he and his wife were able to flee to Spain and then to Portugal, from where they sailed to New York: to remain in France with a Jewish wife would have been courting disaster, and indeed Lise Jules-Romains's mother perished in an extermination camp. On hearing General de Gaulle's appeal to Frenchmen, Romains immediately offered his support, making numerous broadcasts to the French people, attacking the collaborationist Vichy régime, and passionately urging the cause of Free France. His literary activity continued, parallel to this patriotic activity; and his travels took him twice to Canada before he made his home in Mexico City in 1942. There he remained until Spring, 1945, when he first saw French soil after five years of exile. Later the same year, he returned to Mexico, and after a South American tour, made his final move back to France in late 1946, in time for his official reception in the French Academy, to which he had been elected in his absence earlier in the same year.

II *Political Writings*

Concurrently with *Les Hommes de Bonne Volonté*, which we shall treat in a separate chapter, Romains produced numerous other books, largely on political matters.

Problèmes européens (1933), is a reprint of *Problèmes d'aujourd'hui*, less the Rodin/Maillol piece, together with three new essays. *France, Europe, Angleterre* is an attempt to improve Anglo-French understanding, in the face of a resurgent Germany. *De la misère à la dictature* describes visits to Germany, Hungary, and Austria in Summer, 1932, before the Nazi takeover. He notes that the middle classes were impoverished, rather than the proletariat, and concludes that, since the middle classes are the chief prop of democracy, this situation can only lead to dictatorship, either a Communist revolution or a Fascist coup. The latter prediction was of course rapidly fulfilled in Germany. The final essay, *La Crise du marxisme*, is the most interesting, containing an extensive and still valid critique of Marxism. Romains comments that Marxism is the only one of the theoretical structures of its era still believed in—unlike contemporary scientific theories. Yet it is not a question of rational belief, but of quasi-religious faith. No development has taken place in Marxist theory except in techniques of seizing power; it ignores psychological and ideological factors in social development and Marx's forecasts were largely wrong. Revolution succeeded only in the most unlikely country, Russia, while he only considered the urban proletariat, not agricultural or office workers. For Romains, the dictatorship of the proletariat would merely imply absurdities like the janitor reorganizing the teaching in his school (an idea which has resurfaced, in all seriousness, in the last few years). Romains perceptively rapidly fulfilled in Germany. The final essay, *La Crise du marxisme*, specialists, technicians and executives, he did not see that, because of these groups' fear of Communism, the most likely result of Marxist agitation would be Right-wing dictatorship. This had already taken place in Italy in consequence of Left-wing anarchy, and now in

Germany, where the working class, despite their apparent strength, had put up no fight against the Nazis. At best, Marxism destroys the democratic ideals of Western Europe, of liberty, reason and justice, and in reality the dynamic of Marxism is one of hate, not universal love. Fascism too can provide the worker with a similar euphoria of hatred. Romains concludes that France should heed the warning, and that her democratic system should above all accommodate the needs of her professional class. What he is advocating here is in fact "meritocracy," which would become fashionable twenty years later: that merit should be recognized by social reward, irrespective of birth or egalitarianism.

Seven newspaper articles came out as a book, *Le Couple France-Allemagne*, in 1934. In retrospect, this is a work which Romains might prefer forgotten. Although he could clearly see Hitler's territorial ambitions, he thought war between France and Germany by no means inevitable. Given the French army, which he considered the greatest military force ever (!), any danger of war could be prevented by partnership between the two countries. Parliamentary democracy must save peace to save itself; while he believed Germany was as deeply affected by the bloodshed of the First War as France, and that friendship and trust between the two countries were therefore likely. Much of the book deals with the Saar referendum, a topical issue now buried in oblivion. Romains's good will is only too evident, but it is difficult to see what his ideas could have meant in practice except a situation where Hitler was given a free hand to interfere in Central Europe, as long as he left France alone. Thus not only would Nazi tyranny and persecution of Jews, of which Romains was perfectly aware, be consciously tolerated, but there would be no means of controlling an increase in German military strength to the point where France could no longer resist, even if his confidence in the French army were justified. In reality, this is precisely what happened; the only question is whether it would have happened more quickly still if France had adopted a policy of cooperation, thus permitting German rearmament without interference several years earlier.

In 1935, Romains gave the annual Médan speech in honor of Zola, published as a brochure, *Zola et son exemple*. In it he recounts his early memories of Zola, whom he had indeed seen in the street, but the burden of his message is that we should respect in Zola not only his qualities as a great writer, but also a great man, whose stand in the Dreyfus Case no less than his creation of the *Rougon-Macquart* series makes him an exemplary figure.

Romains's visit to the United States in 1936 resulted in a series of travel articles published in book form as *Visite aux Américains*. Written at a time when the American continent was comparatively little known, Romains was concerned with giving a more balanced view of life in the United States than other visitors from France, notably Duhamel, whose *Scènes de la vie future* (1931) had created a considerable stir, because of its hysterical rejection of all things American, especially technology. Romains had traveled fairly extensively in the continent, including a six-week stay at Mills College in California, and gives a sensible picture of American society. Read today, the book, like all travel sketches, is fairly slight, but carries a certain period flavor, as when Romains describes New York, one of the wonders of the modern world, or the romance of transcontinental trains. Since his first visit to the United States in 1924, Prohibition had vanished, but the Depression and New Deal had arrived; he devotes many pages to analysis and reflection on these phenomena. Details about comparative prices date more rapidly than anything, and the informative side of the book now means little. An attempt to give some idea of the sheer geographical extent of America is accompanied by thoughts on the pioneer mentality, seen as still dominant. Romains concludes the book with a discussion of the 1936 election prospects, since, during his stay, the campaign was under way; by the time his book came out in December, 1936, Roosevelt had of course won overwhelmingly, a result Romains greets with considerable satisfaction.

III *The Epic of the West*

In 1937, Romains published his most ambitious poetic work, the epic *L'Homme blanc*, on which he had worked since 1925. Here he expands the vision of *Europe* to encompass the entire white race, a concept which many today will no doubt find distasteful, and which is indeed treated in a manner not exempt from racist overtones. Nevertheless, the volume contains some of Romains's finest poetry, not unworthy of its ultimate inspiration, Hugo's *Légende des siècles*.

In an important preface, he deplores not the lack of poets today, but the public's loss of ability to appreciate this art form; and he makes this complaint the subject of his Prelude:

> *Les peuples ont cessé d'entendre le poète;*
> *D'autres jeux les ont pris; de plus mornes amours.*[1]

This section recalls in fact Hugo's *Réponse à un acte d'accusation*, as an apologia for poetic achievement, and equally in its superb arrogance:

> *J'ai quarante ans. J'ai fait beaucoup de livres*
> *Et plus de vers qu'un rucher n'a d'abeilles.*[2]

Despite public apathy, the poet announces his determination to *chanter l'Homme blanc, l'Homme premier, la race belle.*[3] The first canto reechoes the essence of *Cromedeyre*: Romains links the apparently peaceful cry of the peasant to his beasts, while plowing, with the shout of his forefathers, mounted warriors in some prehistoric folk migration. Wandering over the face of the Eurasian continent, they finally settle in the Velay. Thus Romains uses the imagined history of his own ancestors as symbolic of the entire white race. Once settled in Europe, they naturally take to the sea, and the canto ends with *Chant de mer*, a kind of sea-shanty, pointing to discoveries and conquests overseas. The second canto evokes modern man in the city, *le morose piéton des villes du siècle vingt,*[4] a prey to anxiety, tortured by material and sexual needs, but unwilling to give up any part of his existence. The theme of the city is taken up in the third canto, celebrating Unanimist urban life:

> *Les bruits allègres poudroient vers la falaise des murs*
> *Pour qu'un embrun de rumeurs pleuve aux rues silencieuses.*
> *Des autos luisent au loin et montent en bourdonnant*
> *Les belles rampes des avenues qui vont aux collines.*[5]

Here, as so often, Romains makes brilliant use of the fourteen-syllable line. In the fourth canto, Romains treats those Europeans who have crossed the ocean to America, invoking the skyscrapers of New York and the restless migration westwards to the Pacific. This section ends with the *Chanson du maçon,* building churches, all essentially the same with their towers, high strong walls and lofty roofs, the mark of European civilization all over the world. It is the fifth canto which today may strike the reader as the most offensive, since Romains calls on the white man to regain his original "purity," weakened by excessive contact with other races. This call is somewhat inconsistently followed by another Hugoesque vision of universal liberty and fraternity, a message in capitals to indicate its importance:

FIN DE TOUTE OPPRESSION. L'HOMME DÉLIVRÉ DE L'HOMME.
RÈGNE DU DROIT SUR LA FORCE, ET DU TRAVAIL SUR L'ARGENT.[6]

Yet in 1937, the dream was further from realization than ever; in the final section, *Hymne*, Romains admits that the present is still a nightmare of bloodshed and violence. However, he refuses to give up hope, his symbol being the teacher in the village school, charged with transmitting the values of freedom, justice, and peace to coming generations.

L'Homme blanc is a flawed masterpiece. Quite apart from the sentiments expressed, some of which are, to say the least, questionable, the expression of abstract ideas is sententious and prosaic. For that matter, few would now consider *Plein ciel* Hugo's most successful poem. Romains is at his best in dealing with more tangible aspects of life: the streets of Paris or the villages of the Velay, or in his evocation of his *père de quatre mille ans*. Once again he shows an astonishing range of technique, varying meter and rhythm according to the immediate subject matter. And although he falls short of Hugo's epic qualities, nevertheless he is one of the few poets of this century even to have attempted what he considers the supreme poetic genre.

IV   *The Shadow of War*

Pour l'esprit et la liberté (1937) reproduces Romains's Presidential address to the P.E.N. Congresses of 1936 in Buenos Aires and 1937 in Paris. Romains's high view of the function of the writer clearly led him to overrate the effective influence of the P.E.N. Movement. Most of what he says is unexceptionable, because trite: that man's spiritual development has not accompanied his material and technological improvement, or that writers should avoid national passions. Yet reality is not so simple, and Romains, within three years, would precisely mobilize his powers on behalf of the Allied cause. The most interesting statement is a description of the collective passions of the 1930's in terms of Unanimism. This is somewhat disingenuous, but Romains wishes to save his concept of Unanimism by redefining it. Belief in individualism he still regards as untenable; what is needed is "a conscious Unanimism, open to light and reason, aware of its motives and its dangers, capable of criticism and of freedom, in short, Unanimism aimed at the mind."[7] Yet this redefined Unanimism is scarcely compatible with the formulations of the 1900's where spontaneity and intuition, unconscious rather than conscious qualities, were paramount.

Further speeches were reprinted in *Cela dépend de vous* (1939), the title referring to the possibility of war. These four speeches, delivered in late 1938, make sorry reading today. Romains justifies the Munich agreement to World War I veterans, claiming that war has been prevented, not merely delayed. There will be no enthusiasm for war as long as there are *anciens combattants*. In retrospect, this is the type of speech, weakening the French will to fight, which could only lead to disaster. A radio broadcast of November 24, 1938, when a general strike was threatened, makes an appeal for internal solidarity, since labor agitation and governmental instability can only weaken France still further. A further pro-Munich piece, an article reprinted from *Paris-Soir*, is followed by a lecture on *Les Chances qui nous restent*, where Romains analyzes the mistakes made in French policy towards Germany. Clutching at a straw, he looks hopefully at the development of the French Empire which might act as a counterweight to metropolitan weakness. In practice, of course, Romains was floundering no less than any French politician of the period, and it is charitable to leave it at that. He had the advantage of hindsight in *Ce qu'un écrivain pense de la situation*, an address delivered at the American Club in Paris in April, 1940. Here Romains distinguishes between 1914 and 1940: while the First War was an unnecessary catastrophe, in the Second, justice lies on the Allied side, and if any civilized values are to be preserved, Germany must be beaten. We may feel that this simple message is what all Romains's political activity should have been directed to from the very beginning of Nazi power in Germany.

Perhaps Romains's most surprising production is *Sept Mystères du Destin de l'Europe*, published in New York in 1940, which, although nominally an examination of the "mystery" of such figures as the French Premier, Daladier, the King of the Belgians, or the German Foreign Minister, Ribbentrop, is in fact a self-justification. (An English translation came out in 1941, but Romains, no doubt wisely, never reprinted the work on his return to France after the War.) Although Romains did not view his actions in the 1930's as overtly political, he certainly shared one quality with the typical politician, a reluctance to admit he was ever wrong. The tone of the book is shrill, and at times Romains appears to view the outbreak of war and the French collapse of 1940 more in terms of personal betrayal than of a devastating national calamity. The intrusive note of vanity weakens the argument: Romains begins by describing his unique position in the world of the 1930's, a trusted friend of leading political figures, his integrity absolute and unquestioned. He even compares himself to the Zola of *J'accuse*, or an Anatole France with the added quality of being an intimate of statesmen. With naïve pride, he relates how he "conspired" with five kings to preserve peace in the world; or how the French generals of 1939, having read *Verdun*, felt that any man who could write this was no rank amateur in war; or again how Yvon Delbos owed his post as Foreign Minister to Romains's intrigues on his behalf.

Romains disclaims political ambitions in 1934, although he tells how many politicians felt he should be granted power, and how his partisans even claimed he should become dictator. As a result, the Nazis saw Romains as a possible leader of a future France. This last claim contains more than a grain of truth. One of the Germans who maintained a warm relationship with Romains around 1934 was Otto Abetz, later to become German Ambassador to Vichy France; Romains complains bitterly that Abetz deceived him in his passionate advocacy of Franco-German friendship. In reality, there seems little doubt that Abetz and others recognized Romains's weak point, and played on his vanity with constant flattery; he had only himself to blame if he was taken in. Again, though he played some role as intermediary between the French government and foreign political leaders, this work was scarcely as important as is claimed. Nor was it successful: a mission to Henri de Man, the Belgian Monarchist leader, in October, 1939, lead ultimately to nothing, while de Man became head of the capitulation government after King Leopold's surrender to the Germans in May, 1940. Ribbentrop and Goebbels hoodwinked Romains no less than Abetz. Equally, French political figures, such as the egregious Laval or the Allied Generalissimo Gamelin, were no less ready than the Germans to use Romains for their own purposes, again through flattery.

There is no need to extend this sorry catalog: diplomatic historians of the 1930's have not regarded Romains as a figure of any serious importance. The inescapable conclusion must be that

Hitler's accession to power meant war sooner or later, and that, in consequence, the only way of preserving peace in Europe was for the French to make a protective strike and remove Hitler while the balance of power was still indisputably in their favor; that is, precisely in 1934, when Romains was being fêted in Germany. In cultivating this well-meaning but naïve figure, they knew exactly what they were doing; he did not. Perhaps the most astonishing aspect of this extended political activity by Romains is not that it proved completely ineffective, but that a writer publishing two novels a year, with other literary projects, could find time to undertake it at all. And our ultimate conclusion is the old adage that the artist has no more business in politics than the politician has in art. The belief in the artist as a natural leader of men can be traced back to the Romantic equation of poet with prophet; although highly satisfying to the vanity of generations of artists, it has been almost universally proved wrong. Romains was no exception.

A minor essay is Romains's contribution to *La Guirlande des années*, an exquisitely produced coffee-table book published in 1941, but in preparation some considerable time before. Illustrated with miniatures from Books of Hours, the volume contains essays on Spring by Gide, on Autumn by Colette, on Winter by Mauriac, while Romains treats Summer. This has always been his favorite season, since he finds he can do his best work then; pleasant and serene evocations of summers spent in various parts of France fill out the essay.

Romains returned to the theater in 1939 with *Grâce encore pour la Terre*, a three-act play dealing with the possibility of a second war. It was accepted by the Comédie Française in 1940, with an epilogue added after the actual beginning of hostilities, but the German invasion of France prevented the projected staging of the play, which was instead published in New York in 1941. College productions in the U.S.A. followed, and the play also toured South America in 1946, but has never been produced in France.

The form is a fantasy, set in early 1939. Act I takes place in Heaven, where God has his attention drawn to the catastrophic state of affairs on Earth—which He can scarcely remember. Man is coming too close to the secrets of creation, and while pondering whether or not to annihilate the Earth once and for all, He sends St. Patrick, disguised as a Scottish nobleman, and Liliel, a fanatical female angel, to investigate matters. In Act II, they visit the Martins, who are shown as the typical family of 1939 (even their name is no more specifically French than English or German). M. Martin's main interest is his apartment being built in a new block, but he is brought up sharply by political events when he finds that construction will cease, the block being transformed into an air raid shelter. There follows a strange scene where Liliel calls up the Fatherland, embodied in a war memorial statue, to explain its claims on men such as Martin, who however finds them excessive. No distinction is made between patriotism and nationalism, or between the claims on the individual made by democracy on the one hand and a Fascist dictatorship on the other. During Act III, various situations are considered, and in the most appealing episode in the play, Martin's grandparents are conjured up by a time-machine device. Life about 1890 was far from attractive. The grandparents prove incredibly narrow-minded, ignorant, and complacent, if hard-working, since their shop closed only three days a year, and filthy— changing socks once a week, sheets every two months, and bathing no more than twice a year. Above all it is the boredom of their existence which appalls Martin, despite the advantage that they were not tormented by politics. Although he considers his existence unbearable, he does not wish to transform it completely. He enjoys the feeling of having done a good day's work and then being able to stroll about the boulevards. Such simple joys in life, and man's essential benevolence, are what he sees threatened. Liliel is a typical fanatic and her radical solution would be to take the best men from Earth to another planet, there to live with female angels; she would then destroy the Earth with the remaining men and all the women. God encourages Martin in his efforts to prevent war through common sense, and there the play was originally to end. However, after the outbreak of war in 1939, a war which evidently neither God nor Martin was able to prevent, Romains added his epilogue, rather too slickly transforming the intention of the play from wishing simply to avert the catastrophe, to a propaganda vehicle. The French cause is good and God will not desert it. The play thus ends with the overfacile assumption that France must triumph, one swiftly shattered by the 1940 *débâcle*. Inevitably the play has dated, and should be grouped together with Romains's other attempts in the 1930's to prevent war. As such, it lies outside the mainstream of his purely literary activity; nevertheless it shows his dramatic invention unimpaired.

V   *Years of Exile*

1941 also saw the appearance of two minor works. *Messages aux Français* contains the six radio broadcasts made by Romains between August, 1940, and May, 1941, relayed to France by the B.B.C. In these broadcasts, we find moving appeals to Romains's fellow countrymen not to give up hope, since the Allied side—now represented by Britain fighting on alone—must nevertheless eventually win. *Stefan Zweig, grand Européen,* published after the suicide of Romains's old friend in exile in Buenos Aires, consists in fact of a speech made by Romains at Nice in Spring, 1939. Zweig, already exiled, was then more pessimistic than Romains, who however comments that perhaps for the first time in history, more than half the great men in the world were refugees: Einstein, Thomas Mann, Freud, and a host of others. To this select group of great Europeans, Zweig has every right to belong.

A more complex essay is *Une Vue des choses,* first published in English in Clifton Fadiman's collection, *I Believe,* then in French in 1941. It contains Romains's thoughts from 1938, on a variety of intellectual subjects, especially an attempt at philosophical justification of Unanimism in the light of Romains's own experiences and recent political events. He presents himself as a man who above all wishes lucidity; he believes in reason, but not in the sense of abstract rationalism untempered by empirical observation. He is neither a systematic skeptic nor a pessimist, and although absolute truth is unattainable, he believes that mankind will in the end draw nearer to it, barring the destruction of civilization through catastrophe. He would widen his comprehension of reality to include the "psychical or spiritual principle"[8] and would call himself a *surrationaliste* because he is prepared to believe in suprarational perceptions and experiences. This position is in line with the concept of the psychic continuum, and permits him to integrate into a rational world view such phenomena as extraretinal vision. This point should be stressed: although prepared to entertain belief in forms of extrasensory perception, he will only do so given a satisfactory explanation. Nonetheless, we may feel that underlying his whole attitude is a mystical desire that such rational explanation may be found.

This suprarationalism brings Romains to Unanimism, where he feels that he had hitherto not sufficiently stressed the role of reason in group life. The group is not always right and the individual must freely become part of it. This is in practice to admit the invalidity of his earlier theories. Romains wishes to dissociate himself from the power of the group in totalitarian régimes, but when he makes his new claim that "the adventure of humanity is essentially an adventure of groups, and also of individuals struggling with groups,"[9] he gives the Unanimist position away entirely. He wishes in fact to secure individual values to rehabilitate the art of living, and to make the individual willingly accept his society instead of hating it. Civilization of human instincts may succeed in reconciling sexuality with a good conscience, and at the same time to heighten its psychical level. The "organic link" between individuals is highly important, and literature may help us to grasp this tenuous thread of human unity. *Une Vue des choses* makes a welcome change from Romains's political essays and speeches, besides providing a valuable corrective to earlier Unanimist ideas. As his mature intellectual credo, this comparatively short essay is probably superior to his various treatments of similar ideas in later books.

A speech delivered in Mexico City in May, 1942, was published as *Mission ou démission de la France*. Romains's aim is simply patriotic, and his tone is rather high-pitched as he attempts to outweigh, by listing his country's intellectual distinctions, the disaster of 1940. Necessarily, his argument is somewhat simplistic: he sees human progress as possible but difficult, and relapse into barbarism only too easy; but the French mind has no illusions about natural goodness. He thus specifically disclaims Rousseau as not really French either in origin or education. The essence of the French intellectual tradition, he claims, is the voice of reason, together with respect for human beings as absolute values, and aspirations towards the unity of mankind.

Salsette découvre l'Amérique (1942) forms a sequel to *Visite aux Américains*, using the device of a fictional French professor who has fled occupied France to make his first visit to the U.S.A. The book consists of sketches of Salsette's reactions, together with supposed discussions with Romains, all written in an easy style with comic overtones, perhaps to avoid ruffling patriotic feelings. Topics treated include the hoary contrast between American and French food, wine, and women, tribulations in the New York subway, and the unexpected comforts of American university life. Viewed as an agreeable compilation of travel impressions, the book, though

somewhat dated, is unexceptionable and pleasantly readable. Stung
by criticisms that, for time of war, it was essentially trivial, Romains
followed it up the same year with *Lettres de Salsette*, in which he
allows the professor to round off his impressions. These, he claims,
are largely on the human level; to deal with large-scale political and
social problems after only a brief stay in America would have been
foolish. He does, however, make an intelligent analysis of the racial
problem, and also deals with a theme which would obsess Romains's
later years, the lack of aesthetic standards even in an educated public,
which passively accepts anything and everything offered by artists.
Salsette makes a further perceptive remark when he says that in
present-day Americans, particularly intellectuals, there is a good
deal of masochism: they only want to know the darker side and to
criticize their country, an attitude since become commonplace in
most Western nations. He ends on a note of admiration for American
religious tolerance.

VI   *The Theme of Refuge*

Romains interrupted his sequence novel during the War years
to write stories of a very different kind, set respectively during the
collapse of the Roman Empire and the Albigensian wars in the
thirteenth century and treating the themes of war, exile, and refuge,
no doubt inspired by his own situation. The first, *Nomentanus le
réfugié* (1943), is a *conte* of some forty pages, with a simple plot.
Robertus, Superior of a small monastery in Provence, hears that a
man he greatly admires, Nomentanus, is coming to take refuge
after having twice been driven out of his own monastery in Italy.
He wonders what spiritual message Nomentanus will bring, and
whether he will approve of the régime of tolerant, undogmatic
concentration on the spiritual; but on arrival the older man seems
only occupied with material concerns: food, drink, and sleep, and
above all, security from barbarian attack. Puzzled, Robertus talks to
Nomentanus's companions, who hint that he has virtually lost his
Christian belief, having in the course of his misfortunes moved
from anger against God to the conviction that the deity is powerless
against the forces of evil.

Nomentanus, written in August, 1942, at the blackest period of the
War, reflects Romains's own pessimism at this date. There are few
rays of light in the face of the destruction of civilization by barbarian

invaders. Robertus appears as a nobler character than Nomentanus, sadly fallen away from earlier ideals, but he has not yet seen his monastery collapse around him in ruins. The hint is however present that although Nomentanus's somewhat gross materialism is understandable, the task of preservation of civilization now rests on Robertus, and although there is no indication that Robertus will not also be overwhelmed, the reader knows that its spark was kept alight in just such monasteries during the grim centuries following. Romains, too, treats Robertus not narrowly in terms of Christianity against paganism, but as the custodian of all civilized values, spiritual and intellectual, against barbarism. The result is both moving and effective. The historical story is one notoriously difficult to bring off, and it is not unfair to compare Romains here with Anatole France, the acknowledged master of the genre, for whom Romains has never concealed his admiration. We find the same classical simplicity and sobriety, though without France's wit and irony, no doubt unfitting for the theme.

In *Bertrand de Ganges* (1944), a longer story of 150 pages, the same themes are treated, but the element of hope is much stronger. By then, of course, the War's outcome was no longer in doubt, and a serene optimism runs through the narrative. Bertrand, a noble troubadour-poet from Bas-Languedoc, has been driven from his domain during the Albigensian Crusade, and has moved, with a band of some thirty men, to the Gévaudin district immediately south of the Velay. Weary of fleeing, he wishes only to find a secure refuge for the immediate future. His men arrive at the castle of Lugdarès, but instead of attempting to seize it, they camp nearby and eventually establish amicable relations with the Comte, who gives Bertrand hospitality within the walls. The Comte, too, is a poet and greatly admires Bertrand; he is unable to shelter him permanently, but succeeds in arranging with Pons de Chapteuil, further north in the Velay, for an unoccupied castle to be put at their disposal. The story ends with Pons—a historical figure and well-known troubadour—welcoming Bertrand, with a hint that the latter, a widower, will soon marry the Comte de Lugdarès's young sister-in-law.

Once again the theme is the survival of civilized values in a world torn by barbarism; this time the gentle civilization of the troubadours is contrasted with the brutal invading armies from Northern France. The purely religious question of the Albigensian heresy is put on one side; Romains sees the Northerners as motivated by envy and bent only on pillage. Again there is little dramatic action—and no violence. This is all in the past, and the general impression is that of emerging from a dark tunnel into the light. One of the most interesting features is the chest carefully preserved by Bertrand throughout his vicissitudes. He is in fact the thirty-third Vicomte de Ganges, and the chest contains the records of his ancestors, following a family tradition that each before his death would write a short account summarizing his experience of life. The rolls of parchment in the chest have never been read, but Bertrand is persuaded to open them, which is successfully achieved with the help of a learned ex-monk, familiar with parchments and paleography. Romains's intention here is clear: to give a brief historical view of the fortunes of a Roman family throughout the period from about the fifth century to Bertrand's own age. The founder of the tradition was a Roman count, only too aware that he was living in a time of troubles, but still hopeful that settled times would return. But his son's account is darker still, and a gap of two generations ensues before the tradition, somehow preserved, is renewed. By now the family has moved from its villa to the more defensible castle of Ganges, and the feudal way of life has largely replaced the Roman. The accounts continue through the centuries, with a gleam of light in the age of Charlemagne, but further gaps at the turn of the millennium. The tradition, preserved by monks, is again restored, and the experiences of the Vicomtes become more positive until the Renaissance of the twelfth century provides a high point. Bertrand's father, however, is conscious of living at the end of an epoch of high civilization, and sees disaster once again overtaking his world. But we are left to assume that when Bertrand himself will have to sum up his experience, his account may be more hopeful, that disaster is somehow never absolute.

Bertrand de Ganges, a favorite of Romains himself, shares with *Nomentanus* a simple, slow-moving narrative and dialogue. There is no attempt to reproduce medieval speech, although Romains shows signs of pleasure in historical re-creation of a setting close to his childhood memories. The result is a story which far transcends the circumstances of its inspiration.

The same cannot be said of *Tu ne tueras point*, first published in English in 1943 as one of a group of anti-Nazi stories entitled *The Ten Commandments*, by a group of distinguished writers including

Thomas Mann and Sigrid Undset. To Romains fell the Sixth Commandment, and he tells the tale of Walter Kunhardt, a Professor of French who despite misgivings has passively accepted the Nazi régime until, by implausible coincidence, as a German officer in occupied France, he is brought to execute with his own hand a former French friend from student days. The moral is clear: principles are not enough in face of evil, and men must find the courage to act. At the same time the artistic value of the story, like much overtly committed literature, is slight. The technique is crudely black-and-white; the characters are scarcely more than names; and the irony of the ending is far too obvious. Although the French text came out in New York in 1944, it has never been republished in France.

In *Actualité de Victor Hugo* (1944), Romains pays tribute to his chief literary ancestor and predecessor in exile. He praises Hugo's poetic power allied to virtuoso technical ability, and contrasts his creation of myths which are "inhabitable by all men" with the subjective fantasies of most poets. Despite a tendency to rhetoric, Hugo deserves the title of "National Poet of the French Republic"; while Romains also sees him as the main inspiration for the epic function of the modern novel, whose disciples included Zola and Tolstoy. Above all, he admires the figure of Hugo in Guernsey, untiring in his opposition to Napoleon III and unwavering in his confidence in the future of humanity: Hugo the exemplary figure for the France of the Nazi occupation.

The same year Romains published *Retrouver la foi*, a penetrating analysis of the reasons for the collapse of the Third Republic, together with an eloquent defense of democratic principles and suggestions for the reconstruction of democracy in France after Germany's inevitable defeat. For Romains, the lesson of 1940 is clear. Political institutions alone are not enough, but must be backed by general acceptance of humanistic moral principles. Democracy is not the régime of popular sovereignty as much as that of reason, and the key aim of governments should be *bonheur* rather than *vertu*, which when too narrowly interpreted can lead to tyranny. Romains now expresses grave doubts about Socialism, since he sees the reign of the collectivity leading to despotism, and believes economic independence from the state is a precondition of liberty.

Nor is education in itself sufficient defense against tyranny: in criticizing the facile belief of the Enlightenment that progress would be achieved automatically by universal education, Romains points out that Germany was probably the best-educated European nation of the present century. Education also must be inspired by moral sense; understanding must not exclude willingness to judge. He ends with a call for renewal of faith in the *grandeur* of democratic values as opposed to the "moral intoxication" of the Vichy régime.

Just as Romains's anguish at the First World War resulted in the poems of *Europe*, his reaction to the Second is summed up in the series of thirty-nine poems written in 1943–1944 and published in the following year under the title of *Pierres levées*: memorials which may survive the convulsions of war. The tone is one of dark depression, many of the poems treating the horrors of war and the misery of exile with no sure refuge:

> Aucune auberge n'est bonne,
> Aucun chemin n'est très sûr.
> Mais dormir est une aubaine;
> N'être pas mort fait plaisir.[10]

The link with *Nomentanus* is only too clear. Most of the poems use four-line stanzas, with short verses of seven or eight syllables; although many are personal in tone, in others he brings in two different symbols, the *sage et l'âne blanc* and the *roi chauve mais obèse* with the poet Arbaz. The first permits Romains to transpose present feelings into the historical context of the Dark Ages, and the second, with its vague Oriental setting, provided the basic elements of his play *Barbazouk*; use of these symbols enables him to translate his pessimism from the purely personal to a more significant level. Despite the bleakness of Romains's outlook, his expression is sober and restrained, and he perseveres in using concrete objects as the basis of his imagery, thus achieving the kind of solidity alluded to in his title:

> Des pierres, des genêts, des fougères.
> Les pierres bien rudes et râpeuses;
> Les genêts si verts qu'ils semblent peints;
> Les fougères, ployantes et pâles;
> Entre deux pentes de maigres pins.[11]

Although little known—*Pierres levées* was not published in France until 1957—this collection yields little to Romains's finest poetical work.

CHAPTER 5

Men of Good Will

I   *Theory*

R OMAINS's literary posterity will largely depend on his novel-series, *Les Hommes de Bonne Volonté*, with no less than twenty-seven volumes between 1932 and 1946. Altogether there are some eight thousand pages, composed at the surprisingly rapid rate of over two volumes a year, despite Romains's wartime exile, which meant that Volumes XIX–XXIV had to be published in New York, while the final three, completed in 1944, were delayed until Flammarion could bring out the intervening six. Total sales of the series must now be well above two million, and countless readers are familiar with its squat, heavy type. Naturally, such a large undertaking, the largest in a century of *romans-fleuves*, was not set about lightly; indeed, Romains, even when writing *La Vie Unanime*, had already had the idea of "a vast prose fiction, which would express his vision of the modern world."[1] Actual work did not begin until 1923, and must thereafter have been only intermittent, given Romains's other literary projects, until composition began in 1929. Similarly, publication of this vast series would present finan-cial risks, and Romains moved from Gallimard to the Flammarion brothers, who have published most of his books since 1932.

The actual narrative follows a lengthy Preface which is an im-portant theoretical document in the history of the twentieth-century novel. In it, Romains superimposes his aims on a critique of the novel before him; however, we should not lose sight of the fact that literary prefaces are essentially persuasive and not analytic, and what he is really expressing is his ideal of the novel rather than, as is often assumed, what he was actually doing. He begins by saying that the novel will be his principal work, both in dimensions and in content. He was not in a hurry to launch on his task, since age and experience are essential in broadening and deepening the novelist's knowledge of life and of his art, while he needs to develop a reading public wide enough to follow him confidently through a long and taxing novel of a new kind. (Romains is keenly conscious of such purely professional problems.) His novel will be written in a style accessible

to all men, and treat universal themes. He then moves to the two chief
ways in which earlier writers had tried to portray, on a wide scale,
the world of their time. The first is to treat different subjects in
separate novels which add up to a general picture of society, a
reference to Balzac's *Comédie Humaine* where the *rappel des personnages* provides additional links between novels, but where the
total unity is somewhat doubtful, and in any case not immediately
apparent. The *Rougon-Macquart* series was designed to have a
tighter unity through the bonds of heredity, yet those "laws" of
heredity are precisely what is now most difficult to accept in Zola.
The second tradition is that of the biographical novel, spread over
several volumes, with the general unity supplied by the personality
and career of the hero. Examples are Hugo's *Les Misérables*,
Rolland's *Jean-Christophe*, Proust, or, with the whole family as
hero, Galsworthy's *Forsyte Saga*, or Mann's *Buddenbrooks*. Romains finds such works admirable if the theme is the development
of the hero—individual or family—and he refers specifically to
the German tradition of the *Bildungsroman* or development novel.
On the other hand, as pictures of society, such novels only show
limited aspects, almost entirely from one viewpoint unless his hero is
forced into adventures deliberately to evoke a wider view of society,
in which case artificial devices and coincidences are required. He
gives an amusing parody of this type where *une petite équipe en
arrive à avoir le monde entier sur les bras.*[2] This, admittedly, has
been one of the conventions of the novel, but Romains rejects it:
for him, the novel, unlike the theater, is bound by no conventions.
Instead he proposes a novel on a still wider scale. Using a single
protagonist depends on the view that the individual is the center of
the social universe, whereas Romains claims that the writer should
escape from the individual and concentrate on the group, his real
subject being society itself, irrespective of whether individual destinies may intertwine. He therefore does not intend to follow the
traditional device of the "miraculously chosen hero,"[3] or a linear
narrative; he will switch freely from character to character, event to
event, to attain a wider spectrum of society. Episodes may be totally
unlinked, and even lead nowhere, like wadis in the desert. At the
same time, his stylistic ideal will be that of clarity and simplicity,
to attain the widest possible readership. In this way, he claims
his novel will ultimately acquire the desired unity which will explain
the title, *Les Hommes de Bonne Volonté*.

So much for the Preface. But perhaps we should follow the old adage, "trust the tale, not the teller," and only close analysis can show how far in practice Romains has carried out his program. The narrative period covered extends for twenty-five years, 1908–1933, which indicates that the plan must originally have been open-ended, since it projected into what was then the future. However, it is clear that he had a close idea of the period he wished to cover and the number of volumes necessary to do so. We have only brief indications about the genesis of the novel, but some inferences may be drawn. Romains has stated, for instance, that whereas Roger Martin du Gard worked with a roomful of files and cards on *Les Thibault,* he himself never needed more materials than could be easily fitted into a briefcase.[4] This may be an exaggeration, since it is obvious that he had, for instance, recourse to newspapers in recreating the single day to which Volume I is entirely devoted, and later put in considerable research on the battle of Verdun. Since he was able to continue writing the novel in exile, having fled with a minimum of possessions, it is however clear that, in the main, his natural creative powers, observation, and memory were adequate without weighty documentation.

A deliberate structure is evident in the series: the exact quarter century covered cannot be fortuitous, and while the choice of October 6, 1908, as the starting point was forced on him for precise historical reasons, the final date of October 7, 1933, is simply chosen for contrast. October 6, 1908, was the day when French newspapers carried the story of the proclamation of independence by Bulgaria, together with Austria's declared intention of annexing Bosnia-Herzegovina, threatening a political crisis which can be seen as the start of the powder trail leading to the Sarajevo assassination and war. For the First World War is a central theme, sharply affecting the lives and outlook of most of the characters, occupying two key volumes, *Prélude à Verdun* and *Verdun,* which act as a pivot, while hopes of preserving peace and fears of a second Armageddon continue as a major subject throughout.

II   *Setting the Scene*

The main function of Volume I, *Le 6 Octobre,* is to "anchor" the reader in Romains's fictional world, treating as it does one day in Paris and its environs. He opens with a description of Parisians on their way to work, providing an opportunity to run through the contents of newspapers as if they were actually being read. Only then does he move to individual characters, portrayed descriptively at various times during the day. Wazemmes, an apprentice painter; the actress Germaine Baader; two aristocratic families, the Saint-Papouls and the Champcenais; the schoolteacher Clanricard, and his own professor, Sampeyre, now retired; the proletarian family Maillecottin; Juliette Ezzelin, recently married; the bookbinder Quinette; the murderer Leheudry; Gurau, a Left-wing politician and Germaine's lover; Jerphanion, a student at Normale; Louis Bastide, one of Clanricard's pupils; a bookmaker, Haverkamp; Rita, a lady who subjects Wazemmes to a partial seduction. Most of these characters are at this stage independent of each other, so the warning that the narrative will jump about among unconnected characters seems justified. Yet it is pure coincidence that Juliette, wanting a book bound, should choose the shop of Quinette, whom she does not know. Thus two independent characters of future importance are *artificially* brought into contact. It is also a contrived device that these events should take place precisely on the day when reflective individuals like Clanricard and Jerphanion are driven by the news to ponder the threat of war. So Romains is not so far removed from traditional novel conventions as might at first appear. What he actually does is introduce a variety of personalities, attitudes, and social backgrounds, some interesting or important in themselves, and others which point forward to episodes in future volumes. The characters portrayed cannot of course exhaust potentialities: although widely varied, from millionaires to the poor, there is a preponderance of the better-off and the better-educated.

The technique of switching the narrative from character to character makes taxing demands on the reader. Romains, aware of this, deliberately dramatizes certain episodes, notably those traditionally used in seizing the reader's attention: crime and sexuality. He had already treated the theme of crime in swindlers such as Mercus; now it takes the form of murder, with Leheudry. Sexuality Romains had earlier shied away from except on the level of earthy humor in *Les Copains*, partly because he felt it a hackneyed theme. After the War, in the *Psyché* trilogy, he had attempted to deal with it on the spiritual level. By now, he evidently felt no further inhibitions about treating this dimension of life, and the vagaries of human sexuality become a major theme, occupying a large part of several volumes. Romains draws on a variety of narrative techniques. The novel is primarily related in the past tense, with the traditional "omniscient" narrator dealing with characters as individuals or in small groups. Frequently, though, Romains breaks away from this. Although there is no systematic use of Unanimist techniques, he treats certain episodes in a way similar to his earliest prose works. Thus, Wazemmes and his fellow workers, painting a huge advertisement, are watched by a group of passersby, individually changing as time goes on, but nevertheless retaining a group identity. Romains uses a bird's-eye-view of Paris to describe its inhabitants going to work, while there are collective set pieces at deliberate intervals in the series, here the much admired *Présentation de Paris à cinq heures du soir,* with eleven express trains converging upon the capital. Romains gives a brilliant picture of the city's development from prehistoric times, especially its expansion in the nineteenth century, bursting through successive fortifications and swallowing up the surrounding villages. No doubt the Unanimist vision helped him to understand Paris so well, but immediate perception is supplemented by intellectual understanding.[5]

Another crucial technique is the use of the interior monologue. Although recent in origin, this had by 1932 become a widely available fictional device. Romains's particular interest is in showing what his characters think, not only what they do and say, and as reported thought tends to become monotonous, he mingles it with *style indirect libre* and pure interior monologue, often switching to the present tense for greater aesthetic immediacy. But for him, interior monologue does not imply an unconscious or semiconscious stream of ideas; his characters' thoughts are always rational and fully conscious as they deliberate on events, ambitions, or intentions. A good example is Germaine's reverie, impregnated with sexuality, as she wakes up late in the morning. Another episode which has become an anthology piece is Louis Bastide's adventure with his hoop up the streets to the very top of Montmartre. Romains here re-creates the thrill and fantasy of childhood, conscious too of the appeal of a delicate touch of sentimentality. It is one of the advantages of his wide-ranging technique that such attractive episodes can be freely introduced without upsetting the novel's balance.

Volume II, *Crime de Quinette,* covers three days: October 12–14, thus taking us forward a week. Although once again Romains touches on a variety of persons and incidents, there is primarily concentration on the bookbinder's strange adventure: Quinette who is himself led through a series of complicated events to plan the murder of Leheudry, whom he has at first shielded from police inquiry, by luring him to the Bagnolet quarries, where the police rarely venture. Once there, Quinette shoots him, making the corpse unrecognizable by pouring acid on it. Thus, curiously, the first events to reach any conclusion are those of a detective novel, and one far removed from the idea of Good Will. Yet Romains's intention must be deliberate. In part the character of Quinette is due to the historical figure of Landru, a garage owner who murdered a number of women about the time of the First World War, and whose trial and execution established him as a modern Bluebeard. Romains happened to know Landru[6] and used the murderer's striking physical appearance, although Quinette's personality, his keen sensibility, intelligence, and self-consciousness, making him typical of Romains's characters, are invented. He has also justified Quinette's importance by the necessity to paint the darker side of life; true, but desire to hold the reader's interest through a volume in other respects largely expository no doubt also played its part. Be that as it may, the treatment of Quinette contains no moral judgments, rather an attempt at rational comprehension of the psychological makeup of a murderer, with Leheudry as victim, a murderer himself, minimizing any emotional reaction from the reader.

Quinette's adventure is interspersed with other episodes. Wazemmes starts working for Haverkamp, now a real estate agent; he revisits Rita and loses what remains of his virginity. Champcenais is a member of the French oil cartel, whose lucrative activities are menaced by Gurau; they react by illegally obtaining Gurau's police file which contains nothing compromising, and by taking over the newspaper to which he contributes. Another member, Sammécaud, is successful in convincing Gurau that the cartel, although it makes huge profits, nevertheless serves French interests, and sharp criticism of it would merely open the way to foreign domination of the industry and price increases. Gurau reluctantly decides to abandon his attack, but at the same time will be put firmly in control of his newspaper. In this episode, Romains's intention is evidently to show the complexity of motivation underlying political acts. Sammécaud plays a further role, making a declaration of love to Marie, Champcenais's wife, a preparatory scene, indicating Romains's careful structuring of future events, which will then fall into place naturally.

Much more important is the meeting between Jerphanion and another *normalien*, Jallez; these two characters will prove the most important of the series; both are "privileged" in that, by the common process of *dédoublement*, Romains divides aspects of himself, realized or potential, between them, while their ability to discuss ideas and events provides greater dramatic possibilities than the reflections of only a single protagonist. Jerphanion is from the Velay, and, with a practical grasp of life, is especially interested in politics; Jallez, more sensitive and introspective, is a Parisian, and thus initiates Jerphanion into life in Paris. The beginning of their acquaintanceship is delicately handled, as they go on one of the long strolls through Paris beloved by the author. The theme here is friendship, as distinct from the simple comradeship of *Les Copains*. The two feel a natural affinity and their relationship is colored by the concept of the "privileged moment," and of *vie inimitable*, experiences of heightened intensity to be seized on as they present themselves. Such privileged moments will frequently recur in the series; in a sense they are a development of the ancient theory of *carpe diem*, placed on a spiritual level and tinged with Bergsonism. Jerphanion also meets Victor Dupuy, the Secretary General of Normale, who has succeeded in finding him a private pupil, no less than the Marquis de Saint-Papoul's son, which brings together two more originally independent characters. This brings up a further point: the role of historical persons in the novel. In Dupuy's case, it is fairly simple: Romains wished to pay tribute to a man whom he admired and who helped him during his student years. (Other personal friends appear here and there under obvious disguises.) Real figures of course lend veracity to a fictional narrative, while serious discussion of European political history inevitably requires mention of actual statesmen. To this extent, *Les Hommes de Bonne Volonté* is a historical novel, and Romains has no inhibitions about bringing actual figures to the fore. Politics are also central in a discussion among Sampeyre and his former pupils, mainly Socialist, including Clanricard, Mathilde Cazalis, an attractive young teacher, and Laulerque, a fanatic who refuses to accept historical inevitability, believing instead in the virtue of individual action in history. This again is a preparatory scene for later events.

The principal themes of Volume III are those of purity and idealism; the Baudelairian title, *Les Amours enfantines*, referring specifically to the crucial experience of Jallez's adolescence. Jallez and Jerphanion now become the focus of interest and the novel may be viewed in one respect as a *Bildungsroman*, centered on them and other young men such as Clanricard and Laulerque. The volume begins with Jerphanion climbing on the roof of Normale, a symbolic act which has been compared to Rastignac's challenge to Paris in *Le Père Goriot*.[7] But whereas Rastignac sees life as a ruthless egoistic struggle, Jerphanion's dream of greatness is primarily idealistic, with his passion for greater social justice. Yet even so, his idealism is indissoluble from political ambition, selfless ambition since he desires no material gain, but ambition nevertheless. Nostalgia lies at the center of Jallez's adolescent experience, the idyll with Hélène Sigeau which he recounts to Jerphanion. At the age of four-teen, the two would meet according to secret code messages and wander through the Paris streets together. The delicacy with which Romains treats this innocent but passionate episode and its un-doubted importance for Jallez make it likely that a genuine auto-biographical experience may have inspired it.[8] The idyll was destroyed by an irruption of sordid reality, Hélène's father deserting her mother to set up house with a mistress on the other side of Paris, taking Hélène with him. Jallez never saw her again.

This volume covers two weeks in November, 1908, marking a distinct increase in narrative tempo. Nevertheless, Romains continues to dramatize individual scenes and to record lengthy passages of dialogue with the main forward movement in time taking place between episodes. The reader places himself from purely incidental references indicating the date of events. Two contrasting dinner scenes allow introduction of a wide range of characters. Jerphanion is shown at his first dinner with the Saint-Papouls, including the Marquis's daughter Jeanne and his middle-aged spinster sister Bernardine. This descriptive set piece, with satirical touches, introduces other guests, especially Mionnet, a former *normalien*, now a priest. Satirical traits become more pointed in the parallel scene at the Champcenais apartment, where the recently created papal count betrays a touch of meanness despite the osten-tatious display. Guests include Sammécaud, pressing his courtship of Marie, the car manufacturer Bertrand, Colonel Duroure, an artillery officer, and the critic and novelist George Allory. Here the satire is biting: Duroure, a partisan of light as opposed to heavy guns, maintains that the next war will be a war of movement, thus being infallibly wrong about what was actually to happen in 1914. Allory is vain, lazy, ignorant, and prejudiced, but subject to depression and anxiety since he knows his career is essentially a miserable failure. Another *examen de conscience* takes place in Gurau, disturbed by his arrangement with the cartel. He goes to see Jaurès, the Socialist leader who so impressed Romains in his youth, which in part explains his introduction. The scene, entirely fictional, is convincing, and Gurau comes away with his confidence restored by Jaurès's lucidity and encouragement.

The theme of sexuality is further developed in Volume IV, *Éros de Paris*, on a variety of levels. With Wazemmes, whose affair has come to nothing, on the level of frustration; then with Edmond Maillecottin, whose sister has taken up with Romuald, a pimp; with Sammécaud, assiduously pursuing Marie de Champcenais, so far without success. Again the theme is developed most fully with Jallez and Jerphanion. A long descriptive section portrays Jallez on a solitary walk through a poor area of Paris, the prey of spiritual torment. He again mulls over his idyll with Hélène, and a more recent episode with a girl called Juliette, whom we identify as the unhappily married Juliette Ezzelin. Jallez's adolescence has been traversed by religious and moral crises, in which he tried to come to terms with his sexual feelings. In particular, his relationship with Juliette had to contend with an idealistic desire for purity on the one side, and for complete freedom to pursue his artistic destiny on the other. Unwilling to contemplate marriage, he had been equally incapable of a carnal relationship, and the *impasse* had ended by a break during the depressing months of military service. But his torments have not ceased, and he now wishes to rid himself of sexual desires hitherto repressed. This interior monologue, very delicately handled, is unashamedly autobiographical.[9] Finally Jallez writes to Juliette, totally unaware of her marriage, seeking to take up the relationship again. Jerphanion, less complex in personality and sexually more experienced, is more practical in his approach. Bored beyond belief at a Sorbonne lecture, he sets off walking through the main streets in the early evening; Paris is bursting with sexuality, and Jerphanion's monologue, a magnificent piece of writing, takes on the form of a Unanimist lyrical evocation of physical love. His solution is simpler: the next day he sets off deliberately in search of a girl, and it does not take him long to meet a *modiste*, with whom an affair rapidly follows.

Sensuality also takes other forms. There is a striking scene of Haverkamp in a restaurant eating a huge rare steak, which symbolizes his whole attitude of devouring existence rather than experiencing it. Romains devotes a good deal of description to Haverkamp's energy, initiative, and efficiency in setting up his property agency. In this confident handling of business details, we detect the influence of Balzac and Zola, but also sheer technical virtuosity, the attempt to get inside the skin of a character and to show what makes him "tick." This has led to the criticism that it is not the character whom we see, as much as Romains projecting himself. But this must be true of any novelist who attempts to portray a wide variety of individuals, and the only valid criterion is that of convincing portrayal. Haverkamp is, indeed, a good deal more confidently—and fairly—handled than Duhamel's tycoon, Joseph Pasquier. Not all the volume is given over to the theme of Eros. At Sampeyre's a (historical) German Socialist, Robert Michels, proclaims the inability of the German Social Democratic movement to restrain nationalist pressures towards war. Laulerque develops his idea of individual action, maintaining that political assassination is the only way to prevent war if the general strike cannot. Quinette, for his part, comes into contact with an anarchist group and proposes to the police that he attend their meetings as a spy, the beginning of a fruitful cooperation, protecting at the same time his career in murder.

The volume ends with two descriptive reconstructions. The first is New Year's Eve at the Closerie des Lilas, the literary café where Jallez points out to Jerphanion such historical figures as the poets Paul Fort, Vielé-Griffin, and Moréas—and with a touch of vanity, none other than Jules Romains himself. Jallez already moves on the fringe of the literary world, and it is to this that he will direct his career. The second is a speech by Jaurès in favor of peace, denying that any fertile social revolution can spring from war. He expresses precisely Romains's own attitude in condemning war as engendering not only revolution but counterrevolution, aggressive nationalism, militarism, and dictatorship.

III *Individual Destinies*

After four largely expository volumes, the narrative tempo quickens in Volume V, *Les Superbes*. The title stands in contrast with the book's successor, *Les Humbles*; many of the volumes, even incidents and characters, may be grouped in such dialectical pairs. The *superbes* in question are Sammécaud, Marie, Haverkamp, and Gurau, while the principal narrative treats Sammécaud's affair with Marie, still platonic after several rendezvous. She reveals a secret: a retarded son cared for far from Paris by a woodsman's family, and visits the child with Sammécaud, who suggests that it would be better to send him to school in England, where his intellectual backwardness would be compensated for by his prowess in sport. Later, any peculiarity would be attributed to an English education. Marie, overcome with gratitude, takes the final step to adultery, and shortly afterwards the two travel to London to make suitable arrangements. Later, back in Paris, she confesses that she is pregnant, and that it will be impossible to deceive her husband about the dates. The volume ends with the two deeply depressed. This episode, composed of elements of the *roman mondain*, Allory's speciality, seems unsatisfactory. It illustrates Romains's versatility, but after the intellectual and spiritual analyses of the two preceding volumes, it appears both trivial and contrived, and may indeed have a literary origin in Maupassant's tale, *L'Abandonné*, where a wife and lover abandon their son, who is brought up as a peasant in Normandy. Forty years later, they seek him out, only to be horrified.

Haverkamp takes a great leap forward in his career towards riches. Investigating the purchase of some confiscated Church property near Paris, he discovers in Celle, a nearby village, a thermal spring, once exploited for mineral water, but now almost bankrupt. With the help of wealthy associates, he develops Celle into a spa, becoming himself managing director with interests in the company. This episode carries conviction; yet it too has a parallel in Maupassant, in the novel *Mont-Oriol*.

All this takes place about March, 1909, when Gurau has made a parliamentary speech of such effectiveness as to threaten the government's majority. Since he believes that revolution may be at hand, a more glorious future than ministerial office may lie ahead: that of revolutionary leader, and in a long interior monologue, he muses over the possibilities. These pages prepare the detailed treatment of the political situation which comes to the forefront of the novel later.

Romains's altered narrative technique implies a general decrease of tension. Concentration on a minority of characters introduced necessitates neglect of other more interesting ones, and it is doubtful whether most readers find the events treated here as gripping as earlier episodes. The texture of Volume VI, *Les Humbles*, is more complex, but the main focus swings round onto Louis Bastide and his family. He and his mother make a special journey to buy a pair of brown shoes cheaply, and he is first made aware of the economic realities of life for his parents. Then, Louis's father loses his modest job through a hot-tempered remark. Louis, though under ten, approaches Clanricard and his parish priest, Abbé Jeanne, to find work for his father, whose pride, however, prevents him from accepting anything "beneath" him. Louis then manages to find odd jobs to earn a little money, lying to cover up his absences, until his ruse is discovered and he hands over to his mother the sums earned. The events are, inevitably, tinged by an occasionally rather facile sentimentality. Jeanne, a new character, is another *humble*; indeed the theory of *superbes* and *humbles*, the two great categories of mankind, not so much economic as psychological, is put in his mouth. The division is therefore based on the Christian values of love and charity; and Jeanne may be contrasted with Mionnet, who, though devout, is in his way as ambitious as Haverkamp. Jeanne's rôle is not merely to aid the Bastide family: a lengthy section is devoted to elucidation of his character and sense of vocation. He comes close to the ideal of saintly self-abnegation; Romains has moved far from the crude mockery of *Les Copains,* and is here attempting to understand Catholicism as a human phenomenon, as deserving of comprehension as any other.

Other episodes are also developed. Marie makes her own acquaintanceship with the poorer quarters of Paris in search of an abortifacient. Obliged to accompany her husband to their château, where he has organized a fête, she miscarries in her room, with Sammécaud as the only witness. This is virtually the end of the affair; Marie, stricken with guilt, consults a fortune-teller, who warns her of betrayal. Jerphanion's explorations take him to the poorer quarters in Northeast Paris, and he finds the experience intolerable. Both pity and charity are absurd in the face of such misery, he decides, and only a Socialist revolution can sweep this inhuman existence away. Jallez, though sympathizing, is more politically detached; but he shows Jerphanion a magazine article entitled *Nous sommes tellement seuls*, which has impressed him and influences Jerphanion even more, to the point of writing to the author, none other than Clanricard. The volume ends with the two arranging a meeting.

Gurau is now a Minister; Quinette, now a trusted police informer, discovers that Leheudry's body has been found, but the police, undergoing severe criticism through the (historical) Steinheil murder scandal, prefer to remain silent about this almost certainly insoluble murder. A further character is introduced, Stephen Bartlett, an English journalist newly arrived in France, who describes in his *carnet de voyage* first impressions of France. Altogether, *Les Humbles* is a volume of greater artistic density than its predecessor, and in its concentration on humility and idealism is more consonant with the primary theme of Good Will. If Jeanne is overidealized and the tribulations of the Bastide family over-sentimentalized, nevertheless the volume has more general appeal.

Volume VII, *Recherche d'une Église,* is one of the richest of the entire series. The events follow closely those of *Les Humbles,* taking place in January, 1910, against the background of floods in Paris, and the main theme is that of metaphysical solitude, adumbrated in Clanricard's article. The volume begins with a lengthy conversation between Clanricard and Jerphanion, one of several crucial dialogues. They discuss their aspirations and fears, above all their desire for some kind of faith. The Christian Church is meaningless, a belief in the ideals of the Third Republic too vague, while neither really wishes the constraints and petty factionalism of a political party. Later Laulerque describes his theory of individual action to Jerphanion in more detail, and reveals that he has come into contact with an international secret society dedicated to preserving European peace, of precisely the type he seeks—a somewhat implausible coincidence, and the last metamorphosis of the Unanimist animator. Jerphanion takes active steps to investigate Freemasonry, Laulerque having unearthed a lapsed Mason prepared to divulge the "secrets" of the movement. These consist largely of the superficial details of Masonic ritual, without enlightening Jerphanion on their true purpose. He then visits a Masonic "philosopher," Lengnau, who expounds in an important scene the idea of Freemasonry as a lay religion, dedicated to human unity and a spiritual faith in progress.

Jerphanion is not convinced, his doubts sharpened by Jallez's strongly negative reaction, but Clanricard announces his initiation. Romains's purpose is obviously to show the place of spiritual ideals in the lay, as opposed to the religious, world; the episode marks a further stage in Jerphanion's intellectual development, with comparable decisions by Clanricard and Laulerque. Initiation is the keynote, as with events concerning Jallez. On renewing relations with Juliette, a sexual affair has followed, without however, Juliette revealing her marriage. This, Jallez's first physical relationship, leads to grotesque complications, which copy closely Romains's own emotional life in the early 1900's. When Jallez realizes the true position, he is deeply humiliated in his pride and idealism, and stupefied to discover that Juliette coolly denies her marriage altogether. Jerphanion meanwhile is attracted by Mathilde Cazalis, with whom Clanricard too is in love. The volume contains another long walk by the two friends through the industrial suburbs, discussing, in particular, aspects of *vie inimitable*. They draw up a List of Preferences, a rather puerile activity, where they make their choice of heroes, plays, music, and so on. Perhaps the most significant choices are those of Hugo as favorite writer for both, while as total man Jerphanion prefers Aristotle to Jallez's Goethe.

Other episodes are mainly transitional. Germaine's affair with Gurau is on the decline: having obtained the lead in a work by the *boulevard* playwright Mareil, she becomes his mistress; Romains provides a psychological and social analysis of a successful commercial dramatist. Gurau, now Labor Minister, is seen with Briand, the actual Premier at the time. Politics also attract the Marquis de Saint-Papoul, who intends to stand for election as—of all things— a candidate of the Left.

Volume VIII, *Province*, is marked by a distinct decline in intensity. Jerphanion serves his political apprenticeship as speech-writer for Saint-Papoul, narrowly elected deputy for Bergerac; Laulerque undertakes his first secret mission, to Amsterdam; Germaine and Mareil visit Celle-les-Eaux, now successfully launched as a spa. The major part of the narrative deals with Mionnet, also selected for a delicate mission, to M***, a provincial city where a streetcar company, floated with the support of the bishop and chapter, has has gone bankrupt through gross mismanagement, with the threat of financial scandal. Mionnet's task is to unravel exactly what has happened and recommend measures necessary to limit harm to the

Church, possibly including the removal of the bishop. He handles this with skill and tact; at the same time, a good deal of attention is devoted to a psychological analysis of Mionnet—and to his sexual life, which burgeons into a discreet affair with the attractive daughter at his *pension*. Throughout Romains intends a deliberate evocation of provincial existence, and one much kindlier than in earlier works such as *Les Copains*. However, not all the action takes place in the provinces: there is another Unanimist "presentation" of Paris, *Pulsation de juillet*. The events narrated run from May to September, 1910. One new character is introduced, the poet Strigelius, while Quinette's activities are hinted at by the mysterious disappearance of a *concierge*.

If *Province* is relatively one of the less gripping volumes, it is not simply because of the setting, Romains obviously wishing to counterbalance the earlier domination of Paris, but because Mionnet lacks interest as a character. The ambitious priest never comes alive; while by this point the major interest is probably the intellectual and spiritual development of Jerphanion and Jallez. Indeed, we may wonder whether Romains is really portraying society itself on the widest scale, or whether the two *normaliens* and their group are not tending to run away with the story. This is not to say that *Province* is any the less readable, as long as the episodes are regarded as individual pieces of writing, whose general purpose and unity are not always clear.

IV *The Shadow of Politics*

We return to Paris for the bulk of Volume IX, *Montée des périls*, another long and complex tome. The two perils which threaten are political revolution, in the general strike of November, 1910, and the risk of war between France and Germany. Thus politics comes to the fore, and with it Briand, the Premier, treated as a fictional character, with interior monologues and imaginary conversations. The strike was defeated by Briand's decision to mobilize the striking railwaymen, the source of *Le Dictateur* and a measure of suspect legality, but fully justified in Romains's eyes by its success. He begins with an analysis of the entire background of the dispute, afterwards narrowing it down to the individual character of Edmond Maillecottin, a skilled worker at the Bertrand motor factory. There follows a lengthy analysis of Maillecottin's attitude to his work, another exercise in virtuosity. The focus then switches to Bertrand

himself and his success in developing production, while Champcenais puts the reactionary argument that war is the best way of
averting social unrest, increasing industrial profits and channeling
energies into a "safe" direction whether France won or lost. Meanwhile, Briand muses on his daring move in suppressing the strike;
this important passage contains Romains's own mature reflections
on the nature and limits of political power in the Third Republic.
An interview with Gurau follows; depressed in body and in spirits,
he finds his interests turning from domestic to foreign affairs, and
refuses offered portfolios since his principal ambition is now to
become Foreign Minister. This provides a further link with possible
war; the general thesis, Romains's own, is that the principal guarantee against it would be Franco-German reconciliation. This Briand is
not politically able to concede, despite Gurau's passionate advocacy.
Laulerque is involved in the purchase of a house on the Côte d'Azur,
apparently to be used by his secret society, now shown to have its
headquarters in Austria-Hungary, for kidnapping purposes. They
are also concerned in an unsuccessful attempt to assassinate Briand.

The volume contains a number of other episodes of varying
importance. Isabelle Maillecottin, now a prostitute, appeals to her
brother to provide a perjured alibi to save her protector Romuald
from imprisonment for robbery. Mionnet settles his affairs, of all
kinds, in M***: the company will be refloated and with luck the
creditors and shareholders will be rescued, while the bishop will
retain his diocese. All round, this is a brilliant success, but the
impression remains that this narrative thread runs into the sand,
without all its implications explored. The same is true of Jerphanion's relationship with Mathilde Cazalis: unwilling to tie himself
down by marriage while still a student, he can only make the
unacceptable offer of a sexual affair, which provokes a break.
Clanricard, in love with Mathilde but too timid, is deeply hurt;
Romains shows how even the most idealistic intentions may lead to
damage, since it was the article on solitude which brought Clanricard
and Jerphanion together, and thus has temporarily wrecked the
teacher's hopes of happiness. Further new characters are introduced.
Another descriptive *tour de force* is the difficult birth of Françoise
Maïeul, ultimately to become Jallez's fiancée over twenty years
later. Champcenais meets Zülpicher, a Luxemburg industrialist
with interests in Germany and Belgium; the two associate themselves in France as well, to profit from the arms race on both sides.

Finally, Allory, attempting election to the French Academy, is outmaneuvered.

So far a nice balance has been struck between political events and their repercussions on nonpolitical characters. In Volume X, *Les Pouvoirs*, however, pure politics dominates. Gurau is the most prominent character, as Minister of Public Works and later as Foreign Minister, under Joseph Caillaux. Treating politics, and in particular foreign politics, in the novel, inevitably presents certain problems. The author is necessarily constrained by what actually happened: he must remain within the "facts." Thus the Agadir incident of Summer, 1911, which might have led to war with Germany, was in the end peacefully settled, yet Gurau, a fictional character, has to be grafted on to real events so as to appear to be playing a significant role, though he cannot change their outcome. The question here is primarily one of plausibility, together with reader appeal. Topical events may be of burning interest at the time, but decades later usually look stale, and may even be entirely forgotten. Barrès's novels on the Boulanger episode and the Panama scandal are cases in point: they are little read, whereas the first volume of the *Roman de l'énergie nationale, Les Déracinés,* dealing largely with private events and psychological developments in the lives of a group of young men, has remained alive. The comparison is not an idle one, since this trilogy must be counted among the literary ancestors of *Les Hommes de Bonne Volonté*. Barrès's hero, Roemerspacher, bears a distinct similarity to Jerphanion, and Sturel in some respects to Jallez, while the themes of energy and ambition are omnipresent in both novels, together with that of Franco-German relations.

Romains is conscious of the danger of boring his readers, and attempts to avert it in several ways. First, he broadens his treatment of Gurau by including episodes from his private life, and by associating him with sensational historical events, such as a crash in the Paris-Madrid Air Race. A second way, important for the light it yields on the psychology of a professional politician, is seen when Gurau, though himself a partisan of Franco-German *rapprochement*, is furious to discover that his chief, Caillaux, has been carrying on secret diplomacy to this effect behind his back, and is only restrained from a dramatic resignation by the knowledge that this would torpedo Caillaux's policy. Thus the clash between political ideals and ambition is brilliantly exemplified. At the same time the reader may tend to become confused by the minutiae of political events, unless he already possesses a detailed knowledge of the period, in which case the novel will, because of the fictional graft, seem distorted and incorrect. Either way, he may well return to Jallez and Jerphanion with a certain relief. Both have now ended their years at Normale by passing the *agrégation* examination; henceforth their paths will separate, but first Jallez spends a few days with Jerphanion in the Velay, another example of *vie inimitable*. A number of other episodes are used to break up the political material. Laulerque has doubts about the peaceful intentions of his secret society, which seems to contain Slav nationalists whose real end is to break up the Austro-Hungarian Empire. This leads to a brilliant analysis of the place of violence in politics, and a critique of revolutionary nationalism, inevitably worse than the admittedly imperfect and reactionary régimes it replaces.

The principal theme of Volume XI, *Recours à l'abîme,* is sexual desire, treated in relation to a number of characters, but most extensively to Allory. Romains's treatment of Allory is highly satirical, as in his amusing attack on the intrigues necessary for election to the French Academy.[10] In order to forget his humiliating failure, Allory now turns to perverted sexual activities, including a premeditated indecent assault on a young girl. This and similar episodes must raise the question of Romains's purpose. The justification of sexual frankness has always been that of realism: if physical desire is deliberately suppressed, the novel loses an important dimension. This we can see clearly enough in the Victorian novel. But the suspicion remains that one of Romains's aims is quite simply to titillate the reader. At regular intervals, he inserts episodes which were for the 1930's extremely daring, and are moreover gratuitous and implausible (contrasting oddly with the theme of purity central in *Psyché*). This is of course true of most of the explicitly frank treatments of sexuality which have filled the novel in the last decade, again with the justification of realism, and alongside some recent productions Romains's revelations seem distinctly tame. This criticism does not extend to all sexual scenes; obvious exceptions are Jerphanion's struggle with physical desire in *Éros de Paris* or Jallez's reflections on his relationship with Juliette. Here Mathilde Cazalis becomes Laulerque's mistress, with feminine perversity since it cannot lead to marriage (he is tubercular and his life expectancy is low), having earlier rejected a similar proposal from Jerphanion. A common factor in all these cases is that psychological analysis is added to narration of physical details, by themselves shallow and superficial. This is surely a valid criticism of much writing on sex: limitation to the purely physical very rapidly renders it boring and repetitive. In the sexual as in all other aspects of their lives, characters must be intrinsically interesting as human personalities. Sexuality does not however exhaust the material in this volume. Jerphanion, accomplishing a further year of military service as a lieutenant, comments in detail on military life, while Jallez sets out on a journalistic and literary career.

In Volume XII, *Les Créateurs*, Romains takes up the theme of creativity. Not, as we might expect, with Jallez's literary efforts; although he will become a distinguished writer, his work is always handled incidentally, and we never see him directly at grips with it. The characters whose achievements are described here have both hitherto been of little importance: Viaur, resident doctor at Celle, and the poet Strigelius. In his treatment of Viaur's scientific researches, Romains draws on his experiments with extraretinal vision, trying to redress the balance by making Viaur win through, after initial resistance, to recognition as a scientific genius. The field of research has been transformed: he accidently runs across a former legionary who can reduce his pulse to virtually zero at will. Will is the essential concept here, and Viaur seizes upon it, for if similar physical phenomena can be produced by sheer exertion of willpower, the principle may be extended into many fields of medicine. The difficulty is to integrate this theme into the texture of the novel, since Viaur's researches have no historical basis and his results are not scientifically acceptable in actual fact, and therefore lacking to some extent in plausibility. Nor does Viaur come to life as a human being, despite detailed analysis of his thoughts and ideas. Perhaps the most interesting feature is Romains's evidently continuing belief in the power of will over body, of mind over matter.

Viaur represents scientific creativity, Strigelius poetic creativity. He is closely modelled on the poet Valéry, and the result of his "method" is close enough to be a parody, though it is doubtful if his method corresponds exactly to Valéry's way of writing. His initial problem is that faced by both Valéry and Mallarmé: creative sterility. To overcome this, he simply picks pairs of words at random out of a dictionary and examines their effect in juxtaposition. Most prove unusable, but gradually he succeeds in finding ones with poetic evocations, and by a kind of *bouts-rimés* process, constructs his poem, which recalls *Le Cimetière marin*. Although this section no doubt afforded Romains, and many readers, some innocent amusement, the portrait of Strigelius is in no way satirical. This is not true of the description of Ortegal, a painter modelled on Picasso, who succeeds in imposing his products on the art market at magnificent prices, mainly because art critics, for whom Romains has a special contempt, are so afraid to admit their incomprehension that they praise his work. An amusing scene shows a group of critics discussing painting in ineffable jargon, Ortegal interjecting nothing but the noncommittal. Romains's intention is no doubt to balance his authentic creators with what he regards as an unjustified reputation, thus cutting Picasso down to size. But again these sections are somewhat out of the main line of narrative interest, barely maintained by a few pages keeping the reader informed about current developments.

Mionnet is again the leading figure in Volume XIII, *Mission à Rome*. In this, one of the strangest episodes in the novel, Mionnet is entrusted by the then Premier, Poincaré, with an important diplomatic task, to attempt to counteract anti-French influence in the Vatican and to discover the true motives and policies of the (historical) Papal Secretary of State, Cardinal Merry del Val. Once more Mionnet carries this out with discretion and efficiency, rapidly learning his way through the intricacies of life in the Holy City. What precise degree of historical fact lies behind the mission is doubtful, since Romains adds elements of mystery and scandal, hinting that Merry del Val was homosexual. Mionnet, indeed, obtains a compromising photograph of the Cardinal, but an interview convinces him that Merry del Val is following the best interests of the Church, so he renounces any idea of political blackmail. As in *Province,* the final outcome is left to the succeeding volume, perhaps in imitation of the serial technique of making the reader wonder what will happen next. The purpose of the volume is, however, unclear, and the events in the end lead to nothing. Obviously the Vatican's position was one factor in the complex situation preceding the 1914 War, but not one of great significance, while Mionnet's personality remains artificial, despite further sexual revelations. Perhaps the best sections are quite simply the evocation of life in Rome in years when it was still comparatively small with a semirustic charm.

Aspects of politics dominate other episodes. Wazemmes reappears, to join the reactionary Action Française. Jallez and Jerphanion discuss the resurgence of nationalist attitudes; an American journalist, Maykosen, writes long confidential reports to the German Emperor on the European political situation. (The introduction of the Kaiser is surprising, for unlike Jaurès or Briand, Wilhelm II was still alive, exiled in Holland, at the time of writing, which in no way deterred Romains from "borrowing" him.)

There is no main narrative line in Volume XIV, *Le Drapeau Noir*, but a series of *mises au point*, ending with a further set piece of analysis, *Présentation de la France en juillet 14*. The insertion of this episode in the middle volume of the series is deliberately symmetrical; it will be followed, in the final volume, by the "presentation" of Europe in October, 1933. Jallez and Jerphanion occupy our attention more than in the preceding volumes. Jerphanion, after teaching in La Rochelle, a year he regards as exile, marries, and the young couple settle into an apartment in Paris. Odette Jerphanion is somewhat colorless, and her relationship with her husband entirely *raisonnable* and devoid of passion; later she is chiefly useful as a confidant for Jallez's emotional complications. Jerphanion's marriage in no way weakens his friendship with Jallez, who on his side makes a definitive break with Juliette, whose deceptions have disillusioned him. This he does with more discretion than moral courage at the outset of a visit to England. While crossing the Channel on his return from Britain, Jallez is seized by the vision of a black flag: Europe is doomed through its self-destructive instincts and, above all, its sense of *ennui*. This same *ennui* provokes other episodes: Champcenais in search of masochistic sexual perversion; Sammécaud attempting to turn his sexual life into a work of art. Quinette, with three murders behind him, is well set to become the greatest criminal of the age; again pathological *ennui* might be the underlying motivation. Maykosen visits Lenin in Cracow, introducing another historical figure: Lenin is shown as lucid, ruthless, and implacable. Mionnet reports to Poincaré: Pius X is seriously ill so Mionnet is maintaining close contact with both possible successors. His elevation to a bishopric is now only a matter of time. Romains includes two diverting episodes: the would-be sex life of the dog Macaire, a brilliant *tour de force* of anthropomorphic animal psychology; and verging on the pathetic, the sexual frustration of Bernardine de Saint-Papoul

devant les nudités in the Louvre. On the other hand, the death of
Lommérie, Haverkamp's business associate, has little immediate
relevance but may be regarded as an attempt to rival celebrated death
scenes in Flaubert, Zola, or, more recently, Proust and Martin du
Gard. The volume ends with a short scene in which Jerphanion, in
the Velay like Romains himself in 1914, hears the church bells
announcing war.

V   *World War I*

By common consent, Volumes XV and XVI, *Prélude à Verdun,*
and *Verdun,* are among the finest. In part this is due to their subject
matter, the dramatic attraction of war as a theme. Haverkamp
founding a spa or Mionnet negotiating at Rome has a narrower
intrinsic interest than the cataclysm directly affecting the life of
every Frenchman. But this alone would not guarantee success;
dozens of books had equally treated the War, and Romains, writing
twenty years after it, was somewhat late in the field. He therefore
needed to offer something more than his predecessors, which he
achieved by having at his disposal both the broad compass of
his novel and his Unanimist *vues d'ensemble.* We may distinguish
several basic categories of books inspired by war. First, and this
we can dismiss out of hand, is simple propaganda literature to
assist the cause, *bourrage de crâne* usually written regardless of
realities, often by men with little martial experience. The second
category is the widest: works where the author is concerned to
convey personal experiences which were so compelling as to demand portrayal. In the case of the First War, the feelings usually
produced were those of shock and horror at the stupidity, carnage,
and, above all, futility of it all. As a result, there may be, as in Bar-
busse's *Le Feu,* a propaganda intention of a reverse kind. This
tendency may run counter to the aim of accurate transcription of
events experienced, as may equally the author's desire to over-
dramatize or to improve his own image. In considering such works,
the frontier between fiction and nonfiction becomes blurred; but it
is probably true that many of the best war books—best as literature
—have been autobiographical. As soon as fictional demands of style
and form are made on the material, something of its value as direct
witness may be lost. A third category consists of novels whose basis
in genuine experience may vary from considerable to very slight,
and which may be written a considerable time after the events they

portray. Here, the novelist's task is one of creative imagination not fundamentally different from the treatment of any other material, and the criteria on which his work will be judged are the normal ones of convincing and effective narration. Detachment and reflection on the significance of events will usually be present; examples might be Stendhal's treatment of Waterloo or Zola's *Débâcle.* A final category is the quite straightforward one of works of history. Here, the historian may simply be trying to elicit the true sequence of events; he may also seek to elucidate their causes, and furthermore have a thesis, usually political, to sustain. If so, his work may also partake of the propaganda aim of our first category.

Romains here uses almost entirely elements of the latter two categories. His own military experience was extremely limited. His infantry service at Pithiviers was probably the least happy episode in his life, and medical unfitness in 1914 deprived him of any direct experience of battle. Thus he had to construct his narrative on secondhand evidence, information from friends at the Front,[11] war books, newspapers, and sheer imaginative power.

His aims in the Verdun volumes are clear. The War, as the most cruel and tragic experience of the age, must naturally take a central place in his overall portrayal of French society. As always, he sought understanding of events, to uncover underlying causes and patterns. At the same time, he wished by the very act of writing to help to avert another war: the Verdun volumes were published in 1938, the year of Munich. Both aims had to be reconciled with the necessity to fit the War into the existing structure of the novel.

Romains makes no attempt to deal comprehensively with the War. Instead, after an acute general analysis of how a supposedly brief war of movement became bogged down in the muddy stalemate of the trenches, he uses a single crucial episode, the Battle of Verdun, to exemplify it as a whole. His existing range of characters can be incorporated into this plan without strain. Jerphanion and Clanricard are infantry lieutenants, whose presence at the Front provides opportunity for narration of battle scenes. Jerphanion applies his usual powers of intellectual analysis to his experiences, whereas with Clanricard, feeling is more emphasized. There is a bitter irony in the idealistic teacher, tormented for years by the specter of war, being forced by events to become an efficient military officer. Jallez, on the other hand, unfit, spends the War years as a passive auxiliary, supervising boot repairs. Existing minor characters are utilized, and a few new ones added. Wazemmes dies heroically, but barbed satire is applied to Duroure, through lucky improvisations now a Corps Commander, and whose principal interest is not to win the war, but to further his own career. Through a miscalculation he refuses the opportunity to defend Verdun since he thinks the position lost. In reality it went to Pétain, whose success formed the basis of his subsequent career. Indeed, Romains has even claimed that publication of *Verdun* influenced American confidence in the Marshal's Vichy régime after 1940.[12] Historical figures shown include the French Commander-in-Chief Joffre, and the Kaiser in an interview with Maykosen. In this way, Romains is able to achieve a wide-ranging synthesis of events, alternating direct narration of battle scenes with reflection on the whole campaign. One of many unforgettable scenes is Jerphanion's vision of an unending war, with the armies breaking up into armed bands of brigands as in the Dark Ages, when he and his men would withdraw to the Velay mountains. This reverie, extendable at will, permits some relief from present horrors.

The total picture of the War is not particularly original, though Romains held it consistently since *Europe* in 1916. Both sides were completely wrong about the form the War would take, and equally unable to bring it to a positive conclusion once it had congealed into barbed wire and trenches. There was little difference in right and wrong between the sides; what war did show was human irrationality, endurance, and absurd sacrifice. Romains also makes the conventional distinction between fighting soldiers and those behind the lines: senior officers comfortably ensconced in requisitioned *châteaux* (Duroure), millionaire war profiteers (Haverkamp), exempted civilians earning swollen wages (Maillecottin). Romains's techniques permit him to adopt a bird's-eye view, considering entire armies—*le million d'hommes*—as Unanimist collectives, but without the naïve optimism of his pre-1914 writings. Generals are dominated by events no less than their men and we see above all the negative power of the group over its component individuals, who would otherwise never make the sacrifices demanded of them. Thus Romains's Unanimist outlook, skillfully handled, adds a good deal of strength to his overall synthesis. At the same time, apart from these general analyses, the vast battle of Verdun, involving millions of men, is narrated through some half dozen individual characters, exactly what Romains condemned in his Preface. This tendency to treat collectives in the light of individuals had already become evident; Romains's method is little different in principle from existing novel techniques, simply a good deal broader. By now many of the originally separate characters have become linked, a process which will continue. Unanimism merely adds an extra dimension, allowing treatment of groups as well as individuals where appropriate. As an end in itself, it has been abandoned.

What does Romains actually achieve in the Verdun volumes? His aim of preventing a Second War was totally unsuccessful. If anything, the effect could only have been to sap the French army's will to fight and thus contribute to the *débâcle* of 1940. This is no doubt to exaggerate the influence of literature, though Romains himself claimed that the volumes were prescribed texts for army officers. There remains the aim of comprehension; here, Romains has been fully successful, and these volumes on war may be considered among the most impressive, humane, and intelligent of their kind.

Volume XVII, *Vorge contre Quinette*, comes as a surprising anticlimax. No doubt, Romains wished to convey the irrelevant frivolity of the immediate aftermath of war, but the sudden switch in focus is disconcerting. The bookbinder has by now concluded his career in murder, with an unknown number of victims to his credit. During the War years, he moved from police work to counter-intelligence; there is more than a touch of implausibility in all this, which is perhaps why we are not shown his crimes at first hand. Yet his activities have not passed entirely unsuspected: relatives of one victim have made an official inquiry, which reaches Fachuel, an examining magistrate, who is, however, easily—too easily?—satisfied with Quinette's explanation. Fachuel moves in the circle of a Dadaist poet, Vorge, and reveals the story; Vorge, who possesses a febrile imagination, perceives in Quinette a Master of Evil, and erects a sort of cult to him, without, however, obtaining any admission of guilt. In the figure of Vorge, there is a sharp satire on the Dadaist/ Surrealist movement; Romains's lack of sympathy for the literary generation succeeding his own is unconcealed, and Vorge stands unmasked as a *poseur* when he attempts to strangle a woman with a view to sexual abuse of the corpse, but cannot carry the deed to completion.

Few other characters appear: Jerphanion, recently demobilized, outlines his feelings after the Armistice; already disillusionment is setting in, and victory proving hollow. Jallez, on a journalistic mission in Vienna, describes the economic collapse of the former Austrian Empire. The volume ends with one of the most moving scenes in the entire novel, the description of the *Fête de la Victoire* on July 14, 1919, with its most poignant moment of silence for the millions of dead.

In Volume XVIII, *La Douceur de la Vie*, the scene moves to Nice, where Jallez spends the winter of 1919-1920. Romains re-creates his impressions of the years he himself taught there, in an oasis of tranquillity away from the War. The volume, an evocation of *vie inimitable*, is largely narrated by Jallez in his journal; above all he wishes to preserve the savor of every single moment of life, after four wasted years. Gradually, an idyll unfolds with Antonia, a young girl who works in a newspaper kiosk, described in ideal terms, like Hélène Sigeau. Few readers fail to be conquered by the sentimental charm of this episode, although the affair inevitably has to come to an end. Other episodes seem primarily intended to tie up loose ends. Quinette has settled in Nice as an antique bookseller, having married Vorge's would-be victim. Jallez knows his shop, visits Mionnet, now bishop of Digne, and hears a boring lecture by Allory, an egregious propagandist during the War years, and now finally an Academician. Laulerque visits Sampeyre, and describes his complete disillusionment with the Organization, which far from preserving peace, hurled Europe into war through the Sarajevo assassination. He himself spent the War years in a Swiss sanatorium, where, with his health partly restored, he now holds an administrative post. Jerphanion remains in the background, but is ready to abandon teaching for a political career. More impressive than its predecessor, *La Douceur de la Vie* comes as a transitional volume between the War and further concentration on politics.

VI   *The Utopian Illusion*

In Volume XIX, *Cette grande lueur à l'Est,* the narrative jumps forward to 1922. The title refers, of course, to postrevolutionary Russia and the hopes it inspired. But initially Romains evokes the France of the 1920's, with its increased pace of life and the shallow cynicism of the younger generation, contemptuous of their elders who were stupid enough to involve themselves in war, and possessing no ideals or even ambitions beyond that of making money without actually working. From this, he moves to Vorge, bursting with puerile and inconsequential enthusiasm, but with little talent or even artistic appreciation. Vorge is an admirer of Lenin for purely destructive reasons, and the sight of the Champs-Élysées on a sunny evening simply inspires him with an irrational thirst for dynamite and destruction. The portrait is sharply satirical. Sampeyre, on the other hand, surviving on a fixed pension, is a victim of the disastrous effects of inflation. Disillusioned, he looks nostalgically back towards the past, despite all its faults, and his blighted hopes, powerfully and movingly expressed, mark a turning point in the tone of the novel, one to be linked to the date of writing: this was the first volume to appear after the outbreak of war in 1939. Despair is also Clanricard's lot. After losing an arm in the War, he is elbowed out of a school promotion by a timeserver with political support, and his eventual marriage to Mathilde has gone stale. He is tempted by the Soviet Utopia, while other characters actually plan a visit. Jallez, now in a League of Nations post, meets Bartlett in Rome, and they arrange to make the journey together; through unlikely coincidence, Jerphanion is also going to Russia as political secretary to the Radical leader Bouitton. The shadow of Russia dominates other episodes: Maillecottin attends a Communist meeting, but is not convinced. A scene where Louis Bastide visits Clanricard points to another aspect of "improving the world." Bastide, now a qualified engineer, is taking a post with a French agricultural company in Morocco. The idea of exploitation of indigenous labor is not touched on: Romains sincerely believed in the beneficent effects of Western civilization as the only means of elevating the condition of colonial peoples.

Volume XX, *Le Monde est ton aventure*, is mainly devoted to Jallez's and Bartlett's journeyings. To some readers, this reconstruction of the Russia of 1923, of the New Economic Plan, has seemed an irrelevant incursion into a forgotten aspect of the past, of which Romains had no personal knowledge.[13] His general intention is to show the Russian Utopia as a treacherous dream; the reality encountered is a society bankrupt both morally and materially, where freedom of thought and initiative are alike stifled, and sullen bureaucrats paralyze all aspirations. After landing at Odessa, Jallez and Bartlett immediately become tied up in interminable red tape; three years after the Civil War, one of Russia's formerly most prosperous cities remains completely shattered, and as in Moscow everything worthy of note dates in fact from Tsarist times. Banditry is rife in the countryside, while peasants have been deprived of all incentive to produce more than what they can conceal for their own consumption. When finally the two are allowed to proceed towards Moscow, under secret police surveillance, Jallez is arrested as a spy for having sent out newspaper articles; only with great difficulty does he succeed in extricating himself to rejoin Jerphanion and Bouitton, who are receiving V.I.P. treatment in Moscow, but whose general conclusions are the same. To underline the ambivalent nature of the new régime, Haverkamp and Champcenais are also in Moscow to discuss financial and economic matters.

Before leaving for Russia, Jallez revisits Nice, where he begins a second, adulterous affair (and completely neglects to contact Antonia). With his general disillusionment and increasing years, the search for privileged moments has turned into a desperate clutching at private happiness however insubstantial: temporary "oases" in a world ablaze. We scarcely need add that it provides no final solution: private *vie inimitable* is no defense against the world of the concentration camp. This growing pessimism corresponds to Romains's own on fleeing to America in 1940, but in no way invalidates it for Jallez in 1923. His Russian experiences only confirm it. Romains's treatment is again one of comprehension: to show Russia without distortion or exaggeration, to draw comparisons with French life, granted the imperfections noted earlier, and to make tentative judgments through his main characters. Thus he moves from understanding of events to moral and political conclusions, but as the conclusions follow from events instead of preceding and dominating them, he avoids the drawbacks of the thesis novel. Nevertheless, his position is clear: Communism in no way corresponds to earlier hopes of a just society, and in practical efficiency even falls short of the Tsarist régime.

Romains returns to the Velay in Volume XXI, *Journées dans la montagne*, where Jerphanion is preparing his campaign as a Radical in the 1924 election. His main platform is the maintenance of peace; but revolutionary Socialism is now discounted as a means, and idealism is tempered by sad experience. Since Jerphanion is virtually assured of success, this material is not particularly dramatic. Romains breaks it up with descriptive passages and discussions with Pouzols-Desaugues, a retired diplomat who powerfully argues that France should have preserved peace in 1918 by occupying

Berlin and forcibly eliminating German power. The diplomat also introduces a further digression into crime, the probability of multiple murder by some of his remote tenant farmers in the mountains. An additional scene shows Jallez in Geneva meeting Viaur, now a celebrated scientist in line for the Nobel Prize for having discovered "anaplastine," a substance encouraging the regeneration of injured tissues, and thus invaluable in the War. Yet although this mysterious anaplastine is no more inherently improbable than antibiotics, it remains an artificial fictional invention.

Volume XXII, *Les Travaux et les joies*, again acts as a *mise au point*, though the events follow immediately on Jerphanion's election campaign. He is obsessed with the danger of a new war; the peace settlement of 1919 has in fact inflamed nationalist passions, which are always potentially violent, never peaceful. Another theme is the recapture of past time: Jerphanion tries to regain his confident idealism by repeating his climb on the roof of Normale, and takes a nostalgic walk through Paris with Jallez. Laulerque tries to pin down a recollection of crossing the Pont de Caulaincourt in Montmartre—actually described in Volume IX, in a somewhat Proustian scene of affective memory, mingled with the sense of *déjà vu*. This deliberate evocation of the past reinforces the unity of the series, while several of the principal characters are brought together. Haverkamp, now a multimillionaire, contacts Jerphanion, discreetly making a shady proposal to exchange government influence for substantial financing of the Radical electoral chest. Jerphanion flatly refuses, together with a lucrative offer to become Haverkamp's closest collaborator. Sammécaud, also enormously wealthy through the development of the oil industry, decides to abandon business and devote himself to a life of idleness and sensuality in Tunis; perhaps the choice owes something to Gide's books extolling the "immoralism" of life in North Africa.

In Volume XXIII, *Naissance de la bande*, Romains makes amends for his earlier failure to realize the negative potential of group activity. The main theme is the development of Fascist movements. There are two of these: a dilettante group led by Nodiard, illegitimate son of a store magnate, and the much more formidable organization, almost a private army, firmly controlled by Douvrin—modelled on the historical figure of Jacques Doriot, the ex-Communist who ended as a wartime collaborator. Romains's intention is to portray the irrational forces threatening the Third Republic from the Right;

and although the volume is set about 1927, a jump of several years, he probably had in mind the riots of 1934, which came close to giving France a Fascist régime. Necessarily political events play a key role, and long sections treat Jerphanion's career as Deputy and junior Minister. Much space is also devoted to Françoise Maïeul, shown as not only intelligent, but also entirely virtuous; though from a wealthy family, she wishes to gain university qualifications to secure her independence and is therefore studying for a degree in law as well as in letters. The importance of the new characters, however, remains blurred, since nothing much comes of either Fascist group.

Volume XXIV, *Comparutions*, contains a variety of complex material. The successful launching of the *Bons Haverkamp*, a device which virtually permits the financier to print his own money, indicates another stage in his dizzy rise. We see him flying back to Paris from London, which provides the opportunity of describing the topographical development of Paris, the dismantling of the fortifications, and their replacement by an ugly rash of dwellings often little better than shacks. Jallez is also traveling from Paris to London on the same February morning of 1928, by train and boat; he too indulges in a lengthy analysis of his recent life; despite literary success, he feels something missing. Various sentimental episodes and a dinner with Germaine Baader, where he meets Strigelius, now famous, are followed by a further journey to Nice, where Quinette on his deathbed wishes to make a confession to a man of letters. But the bookseller dies without revealing more than that he is the greatest criminal of the century. The main note struck is one of seriousness: Jallez's anxious self-analysis, reflections on death, inspired by the recent demise of Sampeyre, and long conversations with Jerphanion, now almost totally pessimistic about the ability of individuals in any way to change the course of history, disastrous though it may be. In contrast, Nodiard's circle provides light relief, when boredom incites them to an early example of wife swapping. It is clear by this time that the main weight and interest of the narrative lie in Jallez and Jerphanion; intellectual and spiritual biography thus become the primary theme, with a basis in the intellectual autobiography of Romains himself.

VII *Last Things*

Discouragement is the leading feature of Volume XXV, *Le Tapis magique*. Leaping forward to Spring, 1933, Romains allocates three volumes to the events of that year. Jerphanion reaches the summit of his political career, succeeding Gurau as Foreign Minister; his aim is to sign an arms limitation pact with Britain, Germany, and Italy. However, even a brief period in office suffices to fill him with gloom, in the face of German and Italian insincerity. Jallez, on his side, has reached a point of absolute skepticism, and confides to his journal a heartfelt dream of life unpoisoned by politics. Looking back at the eighteenth and nineteenth centuries, he is struck by how men were able to spend active lives without politics continually encroaching on their peace of mind. He even blames democracy for our present predicament, forcing political responsibility willy-nilly down the throat of every citizen. Not that he regards nondemocratic régimes like those of Hitler and Mussolini as desirably apolitical; on the contrary, politics is omnipresent in them, but politics of one single kind ceaselessly dinned into the ears of the populace, conditioned to believe that politics should be its constant and principal concern.

Jallez's main preoccupation is now at the opposite pole from politics; the magic carpet represents his discovery of constant sexual *disponibilité*, the realization that the life of a bachelor like himself, frequently traveling round Europe, provides endless opportunity for amorous encounters. In his journal he describes a series of piquant sexual experiences in various European cities. There is perhaps something unintentionally naïve about this tardy discovery, by a man in his late forties; and certain episodes are not particularly plausible. Nor does the magic carpet prove a permanent escape. Jallez still hopes he may someday meet a young girl who will be beautiful, intelligent, and—naturally—pure. Again, this "double standard" appears ingenuous.

The volume begins, however, with a long digression, where Vidal, an ambulant electrician, takes a war orphan, Charles Xavier, on a journey through Eastern France. The relation of this episode to the rest of the novel is tenuous. Vidal, like Xavier's father, had served under Clanricard in the War; and at Verdun he meets Imbard, another of his officers. Imbard, sickened by the world of 1933, which he cannot reconcile with the sacrifices made in the War, returns to the trenches and shoots himself. The aim of this rather strained episode is evident, but the disillusionment expressed is in reality that of Romains writing during the gloomiest days of the 1939–1945 War, rather than of 1933.

Volume XXVI, *Françoise,* deals largely with Jallez's ideal love. After his exploits on the magic carpet, he corresponds with an unknown admirer; it is of course Françoise, now working in a government office, after her family's ruin in the slump. As with Hélène Sigeau and Antonia, the relationship is described in idyllic terms, but nevertheless appears contrived and artificial. Françoise is too perfect, and her earlier appearance too obviously a preparation for her meeting with Jallez, rapidly followed by an engagement. That the episode is autobiographical is not to the point, since the effect on the reader is altogether too sugary.

We see other important events, notably Jerphanion's resignation as Foreign Minister and the crash of Haverkamp. Bankrupt after having grossly overreached himself, and unable to obtain help from the government, he stages a fake suicide. Supposedly he jumps out of his plane in mid-Channel, but in reality flees to Dubrovnik with a mistress. This news arrives in the French Cabinet at the point when Jerphanion, convinced of the failure of his four-power pact, offers his resignation. As a result, the significance of his action is lost in the Haverkamp scandal, while malicious tongues insinuate that his resignation was forced by implication in the millionaire's activities. Further episodes bring back other characters. A street in Montmartre has been named after Sampeyre; Jallez makes a speech at the inauguration at which Jerphanion and Clanricard, finally promoted head of a school, are present. Duroure is dabbling in politics of the extreme Right, a kind of Pétain *avant la lettre*; Maillecottin is not impressed by a servile speech of Claude Vorge, now a paid Communist propagandist. At this point, all the major events Romains wishes to treat have been covered, and it merely remains to him to draw his narrative to a close.

The final volume, *Le 7 octobre*, in several respects mirrors the first, covering a period of twenty-four hours, and certain episodes are intentionally placed as pendants. For example, the first section is again entitled "Par un joli matin Paris descend au travail," and the transportation habits of Parisians are noted in the same Unanimist style. *Présentation de l'Europe en octobre 1933* is in fact an extended analysis of the entire history of European civilization, its enormous merits, its weaknesses, and the present menace of Nazi Germany, Fascist Italy, and Communist Russia. It represents Romains's expression of faith, despite everything, in the destiny of Europe; he has scant respect for other forms of civilization, and above all a blind spot for the Orient. Using terms not in themselves original, he identifies an "Apollinian" element representing the spiritual ideal of the Occident, embodied in the various art forms, and a "Promethian" urge, which has brought forth modern technology. Both of these came to their full fruition in the glorious century of peace between Waterloo and 1914. By 1933, the Continent is far from having recovered; Romains, with the experience of the next ten years behind him, can write with prophetic lucidity.

Apart from these general sections, he is mainly concerned with tying up loose ends, and with ending the series with a final example of *vie inimitable*, a bibulous dinner attended by Jerphanion and his wife, Jallez and Françoise, and Bartlett. Once again, the *camaraderie lyrique*, to use a term from *Les Copains*, provides a suitable final note, and in this way, the increasing atmosphere of discouragement, verging on despair, is temporarily dispelled, in this "oasis" in time. We also have final glimpses of other characters. Gurau is invited to lunch by Mionnet, now Archbishop of Tours; Haverkamp, alias Hautpetit, walks around the walls of Dubrovnik; Louis Bastide drives from Rabat to Marrakesh, contented in his colonial post; Maillecottin is now foreman in his motor plant. Sammécaud, sated with heterosexuality in a Tunisian Lotus-land, has turned to pederasty. Clanricard, who more than any other character has drunk the cup of bitterness, once again talks to his pupils about the dangers of war; life has given him little, but his ideals, though battered, remain the same. Thus Romains manages to contrive a reasonably neat ending. The problem of ending a novel has of course always been difficult. The traditional happy ending rarely satisfies the contemporary reader, who nevertheless usually prefers loose ends to be dealt with satisfactorily. Yet the novelist has to terminate his narrative at some arbitrary point in time, which inevitably leaves the future to some extent open (barring wiping out the major characters in some general catastrophe, as in Martin du Gard's *Les Thibault*). Inevitably, a number of fascinating questions are unanswered. How will Jallez's marriage work out? Is Jerphanion's political career finished? Above all, what would the effect of World War II be on the different characters? But these are of course

unanswerable and it is idle to speculate. We can only admire the
staying power of the author who admits that, on occasion, wearying
of his gigantic task, he contemplated abandonment, but ultimately
succeeded in bringing his novel to a close.

What, in the end, does Romains's novel amount to? Despite the
Preface, we can now see it not as a new kind of novel, but standing
firmly in the tradition of Balzac and Zola. Romains is more conscious
of society as a collectivity, but his achievement, no less than theirs, is
to portray *individual* destinies against the collective backcloth. Like
them, he has the merit of showing characters in their daily work, not
merely in their leisure; like them, he piles up facts and technical
know-how to add substance to simple narration of events. To some
extent Romains possesses the faults of his virtues. His great gift is the
pedagogical one of lucid exposition, illuminating every topic he
treats; but as a consequence, relatively little of the novel is dramatically narrated, and the reader may feel swamped with analytical
passages. Having reflected deeply on all kinds of questions, Romains
makes comments which are always intelligent, but his very readiness
to introduce them gives him a tendency to prolixity. His preferred
narrative mode is the interior monologue, then dialogue; direct
narration of action comes third, and as a result, entire episodes are
represented indirectly and therefore less vividly. Furthermore, since
interior monologue is always conscious, the characters' unconscious
motives tend to be obscured. It has been a frequent and often valid
criticism that Romains's psychology is too rational, that characters,
cerebrally conceived, think instead of feeling. Constant self-analysis,
perfectly appropriate for Jallez and Jerphanion, is less so for
Maillecottin or Haverkamp. As a result, all the characters are
tinted with a selfconsciousness which tends to artifice.

In any case, Romains's characterization is not uniformly successful. His desire to emulate Balzac in the creation of literally thousands
of fictional personages inevitably means that many, perhaps most,
remain shadowy figures, scarcely more than names. Like many
male novelists, he has difficulty in creating convincing women
characters: Françoise, Antonia, and Marie de Champcenais are
equally colorless. Exceptions are perhaps Germaine and Juliette,
which leads to the reflection that many of the more interesting
figures are indeed men of not-so-Good-Will: Quinette, Haverkamp,
or Allory. It is, of course, axiomatic that virtuous characters are the
most difficult to portray, and Romains arrives at the usual solution

of setting his morally most admirable figures against a background of failure. Clanricard is the clearest example. In other cases, he reproduces the complexity of human personality in his protagonists. Although Jallez remains largely a passive observer of events, his nature contains elements of egoism and ambition, this latter quality also dominating the more energetic Jerphanion. In both we at times discern a certain contempt for those of their fellowmen who are less favored in intelligence or educational opportunity. Jallez in particular is privileged in receiving a timely gift from an uncle which relieves him of the necessity of teaching, and even more in avoiding active war service. This contradiction between belief in the brotherhood of man and the necessity of an élite is never resolved. Romains departs from the Balzacian model in another respect: physical description of characters is relatively rare, which increases the impression of abstraction. We do not really know what many of the characters, even Jallez, look like. Without indulging in pages of physical description each time a new character is introduced, Romains could have rendered the figures he treats more immediately present by selective description. That this he was well able to do we see from, say, his sketch of Chennevière.[14]

The themes of ambition and its concomitant, failure, are traditional in the French novel, and in his emphasis on them, Romains underlines his place in that tradition. Equally, the belief in privileged moments may be traced back, through Bergson, Proust, and Gide's *Nourritures terrestres* to nineteenth-century models, the quickened consciousness of Aestheticism or even Romantic intensity. The individual rather than collective emphasis is clear.

Les Hommes de Bonne Volonté is in essence a *roman-somme*, the most impressive example of the genre. The Naturalist "slice of life" has been expanded to massive proportions, embracing the portrayal of an entire epoch. Romains's greatest achievement is the comprehension, not mere reproduction of reality, scrutinized by a robust critical intelligence, and expressed in sturdy but lucid prose. He in no way subscribes to the fashionable view that a world incoherent in content can only be represented in a work of art incoherent in form. Romains's style develops more from Maupassant and Anatole France than Balzac and Zola; he uses the ordinary vocabulary of the educated man, avoiding slang and jargon: the transparent *style uni* of the novelist whose primary concern is communication. The multivolume novel produces difficulties through its sheer bulk, and Romains's technique increases the difficulty. The number of unrelated characters and events a reader can take a full interest in are finite. This very range, an undoubted quality, carries the corresponding drawback of diffusion of interest, a danger increased by the episodic form. No doubt the novel is flawed, but we should not let these obscure its very positive merits as the most solid and thorough portrait of French life in an epoch now rapidly receding into oblivion.

CHAPTER 6

Later Years

I The Shadow of Pessimism

IF Romains during the War years recalls Hugo the exile from the
Second Empire, we may also see an echo of Hugo's last years as
the Grand Old Man of French literature in Romains's career since
his return to France in 1946. He entered with zest into his duties as
Academician, as one of the most distinguished and most active members. In his sumptuous apartment overlooking the Seine and on his
estate in Touraine, he led the life of an intellectual aristocrat. Above
all, he did not let increasing age diminish his enormous productivity:
over thirty volumes bear witness to his constant labors since 1946,
no mean performance for a man already sixty. From 1953, he also
acted as political commentator in the newspaper *L'Aurore*, writing
hardhitting weekly articles no less effective than François Mauriac's
Bloc-notes, or more recently Raymond Aron in *Le Figaro*. Romains
continued to travel, at a slower tempo, but in 1953 made an extended
visit to the Orient, his first. Sensitivity to Oriental civilization formed
something of a blind spot in his culture; a similar journey undertaken twenty or thirty years earlier might have opened new vistas in
his work. The postwar years have seen several of his plays enter the
repertoire of the Comédie Française and elsewhere, while other
works, notably *Knock*, became popular school texts. Romains was
now at the apogee of his fame.

Yet behind this honored career, we detect a good deal of disillusionment, even dissatisfaction, not with his work, but with its
reception. He still felt very strongly that his work on extraretinal
vision was valid, deserving wide recognition instead of condescend-
ing oblivion. Although he received honors beyond the norm and
showed little reluctance to enjoy them, he never obtained the Goncourt Prize, though he came near it twice. Nor did Martin du Gard,
Gide, Mauriac, Camus or Sartre, but all these gained instead the
supreme accolade of the Nobel Prize. Yet Romains's international
standing as a writer is as high as at least some of these, and the
range of his creative abilities more impressive still. (Once current

enthusiasms have run their course, can it really be said that Camus's relatively slim output overshadows the *œuvre* of Romains, or even of Duhamel?) Perhaps because of this, he may have felt that the finest reward of all passed him by. And in his closing years he suffered the inevitable yet saddening experience of those who achieve great age; few of his early friends were still alive, and he was virtually the last survivor of his literary generation.

Above all, the postwar world, under the shadow of the mushroom cloud, with the threatened disintegration of all the values Romains held most dear, produced a dark mood of pessimism. This was not the world to which he had looked forward joyously as a young man, and it is no real answer that he had been singularly privileged, far more than he realized, simply by living in *la belle époque* before Europe destroyed itself. Nor was it the world he labored for in the 1930's; that many of his efforts now look misguided in no way impugns their sincerity. All this was undoubtedly at the core of Romains's disillusionment, and how could one refute him? As so often, the last word lies with him, in his wry comment that in the light of universal history, the whole evolution of life on earth, cul- minating in man, and its inevitable ultimate extinction through interstellar cataclysm, will appear as the briefest speck in time, and that no current political calamity can matter the slightest in com- parison.

II *Return of the Master*

Romains's first book on his return to France in 1946, *Le Colloque de novembre*, consists of his speech of reception in the Académie Française, together with Duhamel's welcoming reply. His principal topic is precisely the contrast between the glowing optimism of his youth and the experience of maturity. He no longer believes in a "benevolent fatality," and sees the exercise of reason and liberty man's only defense against his tendency towards violence and fanaticism.

Romains continued his medieval vein in *L'An Mil,* a play written in Mexico and staged in Paris in 1947. The theme is the widespread belief that the year 1000 would herald the Day of Judgment. Set in rural France, the play begins in A.D. 998 when a canon, Carcaille, who wishes to build a monastery, starts to buy up property cheaply, the townspeople preferring to sell and enjoy life since destruction appears certain. Carcaille is aided by a Jew who advances him the necessary funds: not being a Christian, he is immune to the rumor. By the last day of A. D. 999, Carcaille owns two-thirds of the local property, but seized with panic, confesses himself to the parish priest, Père Joust, and abandons to Joust all his title deeds. Meanwhile, in the castle, the Countess, her niece, and their lovers are awaiting the end in tranquillity, comforted by Manichean ideas introduced from the higher Arab civilization. The ignorant and brutal Count has no interests beyond longstanding battles with neighboring landowners, but at the last moment gives Carcaille part of his castle. On the first morning of the year 1000, nothing has of course happened. The inhabitants, far from being thankful, are furious with Carcaille and demand their title deeds back, but some of his gains nevertheless go towards the construction of a new church and monastery. The four lovers have learned a new philosophy, that happiness lies in profiting from a refined and civilized life day by day. The Count, however, rides cheerfully off to fight a new enemy; and the end of the world is now predicted for 1040. The play ends with the confident hope that *l'An Quarante* will be equally harmless. Romains takes up familiar themes here; chiefly the fraudulent *animateur* in Carcaille and the theme of refuge with the four lovers. The play forms an interesting and amusing pendant to Romains's career in the theater, but Dullin's production was only moderately successful.

Another play dating from the Mexican years is *Barbazouk*, first published in 1963, and performed only in a German version as a musical.[1] It is a comedy in eight tableaux, reversing the plot of *Le Roi Masqué,* since Barbazouk, a poor streetsinger who happens to be the king's double, successfully impersonates him. The action takes place in a Central Asian kingdom some centuries ago. Kharal is a benevolent king, with no secret police, abolishing torture, possessing only three wives, of whom one is old and another stupid. Yet there is a plot by his Prime Minister to assassinate him; the old queen is not in the plot, but wishes the king to abdicate so that she can be appointed Regent. Arbaz, a poet, gives the king the idea of using Barbazouk as a substitute to avoid the danger of assassination, and the idea is explained to Barbazouk, who, intelligent, grasps it immediately. He will therefore impersonate the king for a week, while the king and his youngest wife go to stay with Mourad, a merchant in a distant town. At his Council, Barbazouk acts much more firmly than the king and the plotters decide to strike immediately. A hired assassin stabs Barbazouk but fails to kill him, and after a confused series of events, Barbazouk leads a brilliant military campaign against the rebels. Meanwhile the king and his wife, living disguised with Mourad, prove poor assistants at the merchant's trade. Barbazouk visits them and the king agrees that he should take over his role permanently, while he himself marries Mourad's attractive daughter. The theme is that of power: Barbazouk possesses an inborn feeling for it, whereas Kharal is content with a more modest role. Although nominally a comedy, *Barbazouk* is fundamentally as serious a play as *Le Dictateur*, but the over-intricate plot and Arabian Nights setting make it less effective than the equally artificial but contemporary and more "relevant" revolutionary background of Sartre's *Les Mains Sales*, a play dealing with similar themes.

Many of Romains's later books are devoted to analyses of world problems: he never abandoned the hope of influencing public opinion and political developments, though his interventions have had little effect. Much of *Le Problème No 1* (1947) had already appeared in the United States in early 1945. The problem was of course how to avoid a Third War; even so early, this problem was obsessing Romains at a time of general euphoria. He analyzes the genesis of the "Nazi cyclone" in terms of moral improvement being far outstripped by technological development. The world, he thought, also stood on the brink of general famine. This fear was not realized, but another prediction has proved a major anxiety: the permanent unemployment of the less able, who in simpler societies could find some moderately useful task, but are now incapable of exercising the complex skills essential in modern industry. Romains finally floats the idea that there should be a Supreme Council of Humanity formed of the greatest minds in the world. The project remains vague, except that we assume that the members would include Romains. Needless to say, nothing came of the proposal, though he suggested it at various times subsequently.

In 1948 André Cuisenier established *Les Cahiers des Hommes de Bonne Volonté*, containing articles and correspondence on Romains's novel and its themes, including contributions by himself. There were two issues that year, *La Notion d'Homme de Bonne Volonté* and *L'Amitié, Où va le monde?* in 1949 and *Le Crime* in 1950, but a fifth issue announced, *L'Amour*, never appeared, no doubt for financial reasons. The contributions are necessarily uneven but contain interesting material here and there; they tend to concentrate on topical political issues as much as on literary criticism, and have therefore tended to date. The same year Romains brought out *Choix de poèmes,* containing his own selection of his verse, together with three *Complaintes,* somewhat feeble anti-Nazi propaganda poems.

Romains develops the theme of refuge at greater length in *Le Moulin et l'hospice* (1949), a novel set in Burgundy during the religious wars of the sixteenth century, a subject recalling Mérimée's *Chronique du règne de Charles IX.* The situation is more complex than in the two earlier tales, since the hero, François Ruchard, mayor of a small town, is seeking refuge from *both* sides. Himself a Catholic, he has been driven out of his town by fanatics for attempting to protect Huguenots; wandering into the mountains, he comes across precisely the sanctuary he is searching for, the *hospice* of the title on a remote plateau, while the mill is a dependency preserving contact with the province, and allowing early warning of approaching armed bands. A whole society of civilized men and women are sheltering there, an ideal group attempting to preserve some kind of *vie inimitable* in unfavorable conditions. The *Abbaye de Thélème* is also a parallel, and Romains states unequivocally that Rabelais was wrong: the principle of "Do what you will" is inadequate for such a society, which requires a much greater degree of self-discipline. Disaster threatens the community with the approach of Imperial troops, but the threat is successfully parried by a clever simulation of plague, which frightens the soldiers away. All except their leader, an educated man, driven despite himself into the profession of arms, who abandons his men and joins the community. A further literary parallel lies with the conclusion of *Candide.* Obviously, the refuge in both cases is provisional and a determined assault would destroy it: there is no permanent solution to the ravages of war and fanaticism, individuals must attain such security as they can. *Le Moulin et l'hospice* is less of an artistic success than the earlier *nouvelles,* no doubt because of its length. The theme could be treated in a third the space, and Romains draws out his material excessively, providing a wealth of local color, but depriving his story of drama and concentration. In any event, this proved Romains's last venture into historical fiction.

Two short bibliographical curiosities show Romains in light-hearted vein. The first, *Fragments de la Doctrine Secrète du Dr.*

Knock (1949), outlines Knock's latest ideas, including antithanatic vaccination against death, and Iatocracy, or universal government by doctors, preventing war by confining all potential aggressors to the sickbed. A second piece, *Lettre à A. O. Barnabooth* (1950), purports to be a letter written to Valery Larbaud's millionaire hero by Le Trouhadec, suggesting that Barnabooth should give the Donogoo Company his financial support.

Romains returns to the theme of the supernatural in *Violation de frontières* (1951), consisting of two separate stories, of which the second gives the volume its title. The first, *Démêlés avec la mort et le temps*, the length of a short novel, is in three parts. In the first part, the narrator describes the extraordinary experience of seeing, on three different occasions, an old acquaintance of his, called Payelle—who had died some time previously. He had even seen Payelle's body, so deception is ruled out. In the second section, he meets Viriatte, a man who possesses visionary powers. In particular, by intense concentration, he recaptures a glimpse of the past, two monks ascending a hill with a donkey, and further succeeds in transmitting this vision to the narrator. In the final section, Viriatte seeks to explain the Payelle mystery by suggesting that he is certainly dead—there is no question of survival or of a ghost—but that through some shifting of the time continuum, the occasions when he was seen by the narrator actually took place before his death. The principle here is of course far from new: ability to move along the time dimension is the basic idea of H. G. Wells's *Time Machine*, and survival of elements of the past, as in the vision of the monks, forms the dynamic of many a ghost story. But the same strictures apply here as to *Quand le navire . . .* : in fictional form, there is no reason for the reader to accept either the events themselves or their explanation. Serious discussion of the supernatural is better done outside the framework of fiction, when the reader's belief may be sustained by discussion of reasonably well-authenticated phenomena, if such exist. The ghost story itself is of course a form of entertainment, but fear and horror, and for that matter almost all dramatic interest, are completely absent from Romains's treatment.

The second shorter tale again deals with the time continuum, but the handling this time verges on science fiction. The scene is New York during the War, where the narrator, a Dutch violinmaker, has taken refuge. His experiences have induced in him a reversed claustrophobia, so that he only feels psychologically secure away from the open air. In the Rockefeller Center, he discovers an underground world, where he can lead a totally enclosed existence. He comes into contact with a woman medium and a semireligious society, the "Brothers of the Universe," whose aim is to communicate with other solar systems where there might be life. Romains uses the concept of light years, and in the idea that we on earth can observe what has in fact taken place far in the past, he sees a form of survival. At the end of the story, the narrator, fortified by his experiences, succeeds in emerging from his underground world and facing the open sky. Again, the story is unconvincing and undramatic; nevertheless, the two stories reveal in Romains a lasting streak of the irrational, and remind us of the complexity of his interests.

Most of *Saints de notre calendrier* (1952), a collection of critical pieces, had already been published elsewhere: those on Hugo, Zweig, and Zola have been referred to earlier. Other figures treated are Goethe, Balzac, Baudelaire, Gobineau, Strindberg, Anatole France, Gide, Chennevière, and Fargue. Here, Romains makes his nearest approach to systematic literary criticism. Like all creative artists, however, what he has to say about other writers is equally revealing about himself. Thus he praises Hugo, France's greatest poet, for his willingness to attempt all literary genres, together with his determination to reach the widest possible public. Goethe, too, is praised for his universality, while his attempt to capture total experience is linked with the Bergsonian notion of intelligence, broad and dynamic, as opposed to a more arid and limited intellect. The piece on Balzac is also fine criticism, analyzing his depth of realism in terms of the reader's complete acceptance of the fictional world. Romains seems less at home with Strindberg, but pays tribute to Gobineau's stories, whose qualities have been obscured by the author's supposed racialism. His reservations about Gide, both on the merits of his work and on his influence, come out clearly in a piece written at the time of Gide's Nobel Prize in 1947. On the other hand, he pays generous tribute to Baudelaire, who had influenced him so strongly, to France's intelligence, clarity, and balance—at the time when the latter's reputation was in eclipse—and to Léon-Paul Fargue, the *piéton de Paris,* whose joy in the French capital was only matched by Romains's own.

Interviews avec Dieu (1952), purportedly by John W. Hicks, is a heavy-handed fantasy in which Hicks (X?), a brash journalist, succeeds in interviewing God Himself through the mediation of a hot-gospeller. He asks questions about evil, omnipotence, original sin, damnation, and redemption, but not survival after death. To many questions God simply remains silent, as if response is superfluous, but the laconic comments He chooses to make are scarcely orthodox, and bear a resemblance to Romains's own unbelief. Man plays a very small part in God's preoccupations; He cannot understand a reference to original sin, regards the Bible as a fable fit only for children, and the idea of omnipotence as childish and obscure. He had to do His best in shaping our planet with the materials at hand; the results are not quite what He intended, and if the world were to be made anew, He would think about the matter twice.

Romains's last volume of poetry, *Maisons* (1953), contains twelve poems on a note of metaphysical pessimism, the *angoisse* of man alone on a planet whirling meaninglessly through space. The inspiration is largely cosmological, as in *Approche d'un astre*, whose subject is the formation of a star, or *Depuis toujours*, treating the eternal sweep of time:

> Depuis toujours ces choses tourrent,
> Tournent plus vite, puis moins vite,
> Se cherchent, on dirait, s'évitent,
> Se hâtent, mais vers nulle part,
> Vont pour se joindre, mais s'évitent.[2]

These recall, indeed, Leconte de Lisle or the young Laforgue, though Romains's tone of dignified disillusionment avoids both the former's bitterness and the latter's semi-incoherence. Beneath the apparent order and pattern of life lie fragility and falsity, and the hopes of youth have faded. In *Nocturne*, the poet, like Nomentanus, seeks only refuge at its simplest:

> Les trésors fameux par toute la terre,
> L'orgueil des vivants, la gloire des morts,
> Rien ne vaut ce lit rencogne dans l'ombre.
> Loués soient les murs, bénis soient les combles.[3]

But safety is doubtful, and in *L'Incendie*, the poet asks himself if the whole universe will not be devoured by fire.

Romains's inspiration here is darker than in any of his previous poetry. His technique, however, remains the same: all the poems are composed according to a strict, usually octosyllabic stanza form, with occasional rhyme reinforced by *accords*. Perhaps poetic expression of pessimism is more satisfactory than the essay; despite the shift from lyricism to somber contemplation, Romains's poetic powers remain unimpaired.

In 1953 appeared *Confidences d'un auteur dramatique,* Romains's reflections on the theater. The book, without being a systematic analysis of his plays, contains interesting comments, especially on *Donogoo, Le Dictateur,* and *Musse.* Although he deals with abstract ideas, such as the power of myth on groups, Romains, like Pirandello, states that his plays did not arise directly from ideas, but from some visual image obsessing his mind. Thus the source of *Jean le Maufranc* was simply an image of a middle-aged man standing anxiously in front of a piece of furniture. From this basic germ the drama develops, with modifications to cater for the director or individual actors, or dictated by previous failure and success. The essence of his dramatic characters is not external observation, but a kind of psychological intuition. Romains concludes with some general remarks on the state of the theater, which he sees as a precious but delicate social institution which requires subsidy and protection. He deplores that the French stage has been something of a "museum theater," which ordinary people largely ignore, and he recommends a national theater specializing in the presentation of new works of genuine literary quality. To some extent, the Théâtre National Populaire may be said to have filled this gap.

Examen de conscience des Français (1954) is a powerful indictment of the France of the Fourth Republic. The government was even more unstable than in the Third; the enormous effort required to reequip a France battered by war had not been made, while inefficiency, parasitism, and selfish behavior destroyed the value of money through inflation. Romains does not seek scapegoats, but says that the entire community is at fault: the Constitution was, after all, introduced after a referendum. Negative criticism has always been much easier than positive action, but it is to Romains's credit that some of his ideas were to be accepted by the Fifth Republic after 1958. No one could accuse the Fifth Republic of the instability of its predecessor; on the contrary, Romains, among others, attacked the opposite danger of arbitrary and unchallenged powers. He wanted a strong executive President, but despite the American example, distrusted his election by universal vote, since this had twice led to tyranny in France.

Passagers de cette planète, où allons-nous? (1955), was the result of a journey to the United States made that year. Romains's purpose was to discuss major international problems with leading figures such as Adolf Berle, President Grayson Kirk of Columbia University, Dr. J. Robert Oppenheimer, and the playwright Thornton Wilder; Albert Einstein was to have formed a fifth, but died before Romains's arrival. The principal problem was obviously whether atomic war was avoidable; other questions discussed included automation and unemployment, the uses of leisure, the future of the Communist system, and of modern American capitalism. Romains arrives at conclusions of tentative optimism. His attitude to Communism remains uncompromisingly hostile, but he sees American corporations as now serving the public good as much as their own purely material interest, and considers the problems of automation surmountable. On leisure, he is more dubious: the only effective resource mankind has so far discovered to cope with *ennui* is that of *Candide*—work.

III   *The Final Novels*

Some critics have seen in *Le Fils de Jerphanion* (1956), the twenty-eighth volume of *Les Hommes de Bonne Volonté*. Several characters reappear, quite apart from the hero himself, Jean-Pierre Jerphanion, earlier seen in the *âge ingrat* of his teens. Romains stated however that it should be considered as a lateral shoot, rather than a deliberate continuation; since his main theme is the moral bankruptcy of the new generation, it would be easier to communicate this by a comparison with the earlier generation of Jallez and Jerphanion, already familiar.[4]

After a stormy adolescence followed by war service, escape from Germany, work with the Free French and in the *maquis,* young Jerphanion found it difficult to settle down. A chance meeting with Herrard, a raffish and unscrupulous Resistance comrade, leads to a business association in which Herrard, advised by one Hautpetit, né Haverkamp, now living in Portugal, launches into the construction of condominium apartment blocks. Jean-Pierre is of course chiefly useful through his father's name. A first venture goes well, but a second comes to grief through shoddy work by the architects. To pay for repairs, Herrard misapplies advances from a third block, which inevitably cannot be completed, and Herrard and Jean-Pierre are charged with fraud. This is the position at the start of the book, when Jean-Pierre is living, confined by his parents, in a small house in the Velay, a somewhat unlikely situation. Encouraged by his lawyer, he writes a series of accounts of his experiences since childhood, which allows Romains to treat his major theme. The disadvantage of this technique is lack of dramatic interest, though the immediate problem of Jean-Pierre's future is solved by Romains in a way which is perhaps a little too neat: Herrard absconds and the case against Jean-Pierre is quietly dropped. Then an even stranger twist occurs, when Jerphanion and Odette decide that their son would be steadier if he married, and select a girl he hardly knows, but in whose choice he is prepared to acquiesce. The novel ends with his pilgrimage to Austrian farmers who had helped him to escape into Switzerland.

Le Fils de Jerphanion is disappointing. Certain aspects of the action are distinctly implausible, and others irrelevant, such as a long digression on incest. Jean-Pierre scarcely seems consistent as a character, while his dislike of the post-1945 atmosphere and his pessimism are Romains's rather than his own. The theme of the spiritual vacuum of postwar youth had moreover already been treated in such works as André Chamson's *La Neige et la fleur* (1951), and Romains does not have a great deal to add. Above all, the inevitable parallel with *Les Hommes de Bonne Volonté* shows an undeniable drying up of creative powers; for his next fictional subject, he will turn to something completely different.

With *Une femme singulière* (1957), Romains began another ambitious fictional undertaking, the story of a foreign adventuress who rises to the most influential circles of French society. Sequels followed rapidly: *Le Besoin de voir clair* in 1958, and the two volumes of *Mémoires de Madame Chauverel* in 1959 and 1960. The story unfolds from the viewpoint of Henri Chauverel, an idealistic young man who discovers that his apparent mother is in fact the second wife of his deceased father, while he himself is the son of the first marriage. Shocked by being kept in ignorance and his doubts aroused, he discovers that Madame Chauverel, now a leading political hostess and mistress of a cabinet minister, has a doubtful past. Through an unlikely coincidence, Henri becomes private secretary to the Prefect of Police, and a shrewd young Inspector, Antonelli, is put to investigate. Soon suspicions are raised that Madame Chauverel may have contacts with foreign intelligence, and moreover that she may have played a part in the premature deaths of her husband and his first wife. Afraid of being unmasked, she takes refuge, first in a convent, then in Italy.

In *Le Besoin de voir clair* Antonelli sets out to convert suspicions into facts, traveling to Brazil where Madame Chauverel lived before coming to France. Her past is indeed unsavory. Born out of wedlock in Rome, she went with a lover to Rio (at Mussolini's behest!) where she worked as a call girl, murdered the lover with the help of a mysterious, undetectable native poison, and was recruited by Soviet intelligence. Sent to Paris, she soon entangled Chauverel, an unworldly professor, and eventually established herself in a position where she could not only pass on secret information, but even influence French policy.

In the *Mémoires,* a third narrative viewpoint is used. Antonelli, in the guise of a publisher, persuades Madame Chauverel, now out of reach of French justice, to write her memoirs as of singular public interest. This she does, as an apologia for her career, and once more we run through her life story. No action can be taken and what, if anything, will happen is left completely open.

It is difficult to see what Romains hoped to achieve in all this, which, with four lengthy volumes, would provide a major creative task for any writer, let alone a man in his seventies. The primary interest is that of the novel of mystery, spiced with murder, espionage, and sex. Yet the mystery is never fully resolved, and is weakened by Romains's tendency to make all the steps of the plot fit neatly and logically in place. By the final two volumes the main events are all known, and we have at times the feeling of reading a thrice-told tale, with consequent verbosity and repetitiousness. Above all, the series is weak because none of the themes is really gripping, and none of the characters of any lasting interest. Henri is so naïve as to be a ninny, and never comes to life; nor does Antonelli, while the heroine is totally implausible. The memoirs are, bluntly, dull, and on the whole the series seems unlikely to survive.

Souvenirs et confidences d'un écrivain (1958) reprints *Souvenirs d'un auteur dramatique,* together with other autobiographical material related in an easy informal manner. *Une jeunesse littéraire* describes the atmosphere of Romains's years at Condorcet, giving a slightly idealized view of his early literary friendships. *Ce que les voyages m'ont appris* discusses the value of travel for the writer: Romains sees this as beneficial in his own case, but by no means necessarily so for everyone. In the third section, *Origine des personnages,* Romains nails his colors firmly to the great psychological tradition of the novel, which he sees as essential in any great literature. The great characters of literature seem "larger than life," since we learn to know them, with their unseen motivation, better than some of the closest of the people around us. Two further sections deal with characters from his own novels: the seven *copains,* Lucienne, Gurau, and Maillecottin. Here Romains indulges mainly in self-justification, with no great modesty.

Also in 1958, Romains brought out *Situation de la terre,* a fantasy report from interstellar travelers on Earth and its inhabitants. It describes what men are like, their evolution and the conditions of their existence, their means of reproduction, and their various institutions. The tone is entirely objective with no moral judgments, as an anthropologist might report on the inhabitants of some previously unknown island. However, since Romains eschews irony and wit, depriving himself of the most attractive possibilities of enlivening the book, it remains feeble.

The fiftieth anniversary of October 6, 1908 was celebrated by a banquet, with speeches by André François-Poncet, the distinguished diplomat and Romains's friend from Normale, André Maurois, and a reply by Romains himself. These speeches were reprinted in *Cinquantenaire du 6 octobre,* but add little to our knowledge of Romains's work.

Hommes, Médecins, Machines (1959) contains essays on medicine, on the automobile, railways and ships, on machines generally, and on scientific development. Romains deplores the dehumanization of the doctor/patient relationship, but sees the history of medicine, despite reactionary episodes, as an integral part of progressive human enlightenment. The essays on travel are the most attractive, and in his recollections of pre-1914 motoring, during the heroic age of the car, he recaptures the lighthearted gaiety of *Les Copains.* Indeed the automobile then, despite frequent mechanical breakdowns, was completely in harmony with Romains's ideal of free, joyful and exciting life, but half a century later, the wheel, we might say, has come full circle, and he regrets the domination and destruction of city life by the motor vehicle. The only solution is the complete banning of many city streets to motor traffic—precisely what has recently taken place in many European cities. Romains's love of travel is evident in his essays

on the railway train and the ocean liner: for so many of his generation, the train is invested with an aura of glamor, while traveling
by ship has become one of the refinements of modern civilization.
He is less kindly disposed towards air travel, too rapid even to
see the landscape overflown, and consequently inhuman.

IV *The Decade of 1960*

In 1960 appeared *Pour raison garder,* reflections on aspects of
modern thought; second and third volumes came out in 1963 and
1967. In these reflections, some a few lines but others the length of
essays, Romains's aim is to dispel the mental confusion which he
sees as having enveloped human activity more and more, such as
the prejudice in favor of novelty at all cost, and to return to the
ideal of clear thinking. In the main he treats philosophical and
scientific problems, thus returning to the professional interests
of his early manhood, and applying to them a robust common
sense. Philosophy he sees as the effort of the human mind to construct as plausible as possible an idea of reality, and the questions
treated include difficulties of such concepts as infinite space and
time; the evolution of organisms, their relative size and longevity,
and the possibility of their existence elsewhere in the universe;
clairvoyance; and the difficulty of establishing social morality
without religious sanctions. Romains feels that ordinary people
need some kind of religion, and that decline of Christian belief
has produced a corresponding increase in even more irrational
temptations such as astrology. Religion has therefore a pragmatic
value, as a protection against "mental epidemics." In general, he
remains the rationalist of his youth where religion and metaphysics
are concerned, but has become darkly pessimistic about mankind's
chances of surviving into the next century. Democracy he sees as
far from a perfect system, but the one with all round the fewest
drawbacks; but he has little confidence in the prospect of newly
independent states, particularly in Africa, being able to achieve
any degree of tolerant government comparable with current
European levels.

Pour raison garder may be seen as a credo, Romains's considered
opinions on important questions. Their very range illustrates his
aim to be the *homo plenarius* of the Renaissance ideal. His exposition
of ideas is throughout clear and to the point, yet for all that, these

volumes belong to the journalistic rather than literary side of Romains's output.

1960 also saw *Les Hauts et les bas de la liberté,* reprinting three works published during the War, *Messages aux Français, Mission ou démission de la France,* and *Retrouver la foi,* with two 1939 speeches, when prevention of war was his primary aim, and two recent articles from *L'Aurore* in which he expresses his anxiety about the dangers of Caesarism in the Gaullist government.

Romains's next novel again strips away the façade from an unscrupulous career. *Un grand honnête homme* (1961) is told to the narrator by a lawyer friend, Maître Ambard, in 1937, just after the funeral ceremony for the *grand honnête homme* of the title, the highly successful and distinguished Dr. Bruniaud. Forty years earlier, Bruniaud's young wife had just died, supposedly of typhoid, and his mother-in-law, Mme Le Garrée, had disappeared. Ambard, contacted by a distant relative, discovered that Bruniaud had sequestrated Mme Le Garrée as insane and stolen her property, while intending to make a second, brilliant match. By skillful maneuvering, Ambard succeeded in gaining the release of Mme Le Garrée and in frustrating Bruniaud's machinations, with all the stolen funds returned and a huge sum paid in compensation. He does not, however, have Bruniaud brought before the courts and thus rid society of a rogue, who despite this setback later rises to the most respected heights of professional success.

Romains has stated that the basis of this story is authentic, not imaginary, and was indeed told him by a lawyer friend.[5] His aim was truth and simplicity, the concept of truth not excluding an extraordinary sequence of events such as those narrated. Nevertheless, this further treatment of imposture provides little that is new, and suffers from too much static if rational analysis and insufficient dramatic tension. The whole *cadre* of the story, though traditional, tends to clumsiness, since we have a double first person narrator, Romains himself and then Ambard. The novel is readable enough, though with no great depth, but it is not unfair to say that this type of story is done vastly better by Georges Simenon.

The same year, Romains wrote a twenty-page introduction to an album of photographs of the work of Paul Landowski (1875–1961), whose work, academic and monumental in type, is not widely known outside France, but who for Romains is one of the great figures of the age. Besides expressing his admiration, Romains makes pungent remarks about what he sees as the general state of decadence in contemporary art forms: the desperate rush towards originality at all costs, neglecting the tradition of technical skill and seriousness of conception. Perfection of form needs to be welded to significance of content, and at the same time the completed work—in whatever art form—should make a wide appeal to a cultured public. The greatest artists demonstrate invention and discipline, emotion and detachment, observation and inspiration, with of course creative fertility.

A third production of 1961 was André Bourin's *Connaissance de Jules Romains*. This well-illustrated volume provides a good deal of valuable information about Romains, who concludes each chapter with a few pages of commentary.

Romains's last fictional work was *Portraits d'inconnus* (1962), a series of fifteen unconnected descriptive sketches. Most of the figures he treats are Men of Good Will, exposed to anxiety and solitude, yet who do their work as best they are able. Thus we have the middle-aged doctor under strain, the truck driver on night duty, the humble one-armed cleaning woman, the ageing actor unable to memorize his lines, the magistrate seeking to preserve his integrity in the face of political pressures, the unsuccessful poet ekeing out a modest salary by ghostwriting. Exceptions are *Le Directeur de conscience* where Romains aims sharp satirical darts at a hypocritical and self-interested Catholic writer—perhaps an oblique attack on François Mauriac, who had just made an unprovoked public attack on Romains[6]—and *Le Maître-Nageur,* an equally contemptuous dismissal of the timeserving politician. The sketches are incisive, but the general effect is rather of a collection of undramatic leftovers from *Les Hommes de Bonne Volonté.* Several times the treatment verges on sentimentality, and the most lively writing is actually contained in the two hostile sketches, with their mordant irony.

In 1964 Romains brought out *Ai-je fait ce que j'ai voulu?,* one of a series in which authors judge their own work. In general, Romains shows himself extremely satisfied with his literary achievements through the years. As a source of information on Romains the book is indispensable, but as a literary autobiography, it suffers from its self-justificatory tone.

The two volumes of *Lettres à un ami*, published in 1964 and 1965, consist of Romains's *L'Aurore* contributions of 1961 and

1962. Articles collected into book form do not in general form an outstanding literary genre, and their very qualities of topicality and hardhitting polemics tend to make them repetitive and ill-humored in retrospect. Writing during the climax of the Algerian movement for independence, Romains was opposed to the Gaullist policy of negotiation and withdrawal. It would be unfair, however, to dismiss his political pronouncements as simply those of an ageing Allory churning out his weekly *chronique*, fossilized by membership of the Académie into a die-hard reactionary. Romains has indeed remained faithful to the ideals of the Third Republic, and he is not alone in looking back nostalgically to the *belle époque* of pre-1914, and in seeing the inability of France and Germany to keep the peace then as the root of all later political events.

In *Lettre ouverte contre une vaste conspiration* (1966), Romains elaborates earlier strictures on aspects of modern culture. His position is one of reasoned traditionalism, and his main complaint against modern art forms is their barrenness of inspiration and poverty of technique. The vast conspiracy of the title, however, is not so much the conspiracy of artists to inflict worthless products on the public, as the conspiracy of silence by the public itself, the decline of any general critical sense, which means that virtually "anything goes" in modern art, as long as it is "original." This Romains connects with the trivialization of any material, however intelligent, touched by the modern newspaper, radio, or television. He complains that many contemporary artists, especially abstract artists, have no interest in technical competence or even basic skills, but merely search for gimmicks to attract attention. He compares this *paresse* in artists with the complexity of, for example, computer engineering or aircraft design, where immense technical skill is fundamental, and sees the same phenomenon in the field of literature. A divorce has taken place between poetry and the general public: he likens most current poetry to loosely executed ornaments, only looked at, not even read, in a moment of distraction by a minute fraction of the public. The *nouveau roman* is illegible and boring, while its so-called technical inventions date back half a century. Critics bear a great deal of responsibility, he states, for not exercising rational judgment and for developing monstrous pseudointellectual jargon, which has now spread to creative artists themselves, who use it to escape critical examination altogether. In developing this stringent critique, Romains is of course defending his own conception of art, but what he says will strike a chord in many readers, in his common sense viewpoint, for instance that *ennui* is one of the best negative criteria for judgment. He argues further that apparent acceptance of current art does not mean increased genuine public interest, but merely apathetic willingness to go along with the latest fad, abandoning the last as gaily as it accepts the next. This was perhaps Romains's most vigorous and effective book in the 1960's.

In his last years, Romains's professional interests broadened to include formal history, naturally enough at the level of popularization. In 1962, he collaborated on a book by various hands, *Alexandre le Grand,* contributing an essay comparing Alexander to Julius Caesar and Napoleon. The French Emperor is treated more extensively in *Napoléon par lui-même* (1963), a series of texts written by Napoleon throughout his career from college onwards, to which Romains contributed an introduction and commentaries, including an intelligent discussion of Napoleon's career. He does not believe in fashionable theories of historical inevitability: if Napoleon had died in childhood, the entire history of France and Europe would have been very different—and better. Romains indeed holds Napoleon in large part responsible for the development of the scourges of nationalism and militarism.

A contributory essay to *Hommage à Galilée* (1965) was followed by a more extensive work, *Marc-Aurèle ou l'Empereur de Bonne Volonté* (1968), where Romains interprets the career of an admired historical figure. Following Duhamel's dictum that the historian is the novelist dealing with past events, he puts himself in the place of Marcus Aurelius, with lengthy self-analysis. Necessarily a good deal of this is pure hypothesis; but the portrait brings out the Stoic Emperor's well-known qualities of resignation, acceptance of responsibility, and humility: a conception of virtue, in terms of duty, unfashionable today but still valid.

Amitiés et rencontres (1970), Romains's last book, contains over fifty sketches, mostly brief, of figures met during his life. They run from Victor Hugo—Romains's mother, while pregnant, attended Hugo's state funeral—to Charlie Chaplin. Inevitably, many are slight, but several cast an interesting light on well-known figures. Romains is no respecter of conventional reputations: he found both Suarès and Péguy pretentious and insincere, and treats Max Jacob, whom he knew intimately, quite simply as a *mystifica-*

teur. One or two pieces are in fact executions: the one on Gide, while the portrait of Duhamel shows a remarkably pugnacious figure in pre-1914 days, very different from the mild and tolerant image of later years. The sketches of Jouvet and other theater directors, such as Antoine, Copeau, Dullin, illuminate Romains's career as a dramatist. That on Chennevière is perhaps the most poignant: Romains thought that Chennevière was unable to bring brilliant talents to fruition through feeling obliged to marry the seamstress he had seduced and made pregnant. It is unfair to criticize Romains for not writing a different book from the one he intended, but it is still permissible to regret that he never undertook an integrated autobiography.

CHAPTER 7

Conclusion

I T is obviously impossible to predict where a literary reputation will stand in a century's time; the most the critic may hazard is an estimation of the value and importance of work against the background of contemporaries and predecessors. We have already sufficient perspective to "situate" Romains in the French literary tradition. Looked at from the 1970's, he can be seen as essentially a product of the nineteenth century. Since the Romantics, young artists have desired originality above all. Romains was no exception, presenting Unanimism as an entirely new literary creed and philosophy, even a substitute religion. Yet a writer's work is usually derivative in its earlier stages; even violent reaction against previous trends betrays obsession with them. In reality no one can totally evade influences, and what counts is ability to mold them during development towards individual maturity.

Thus we can see Romains today as a direct inheritor of Hugo and Baudelaire, of Balzac and Zola, the tradition of whose work he both deepens and broadens. Beyond them, Goethe provided the general ideal of universal man rather than a particular literary legacy. Hugo furnished the vision of a mystical faith in developing human solidarity in harmony with scientific development, a kind of ethical Evolutionism, which in effect represents most of the social content of Unanimism. The 1914–1918 War was to destroy this overfacile optimism permanently. We can also now estimate the importance of Unanimism in Romains's work. In the end his literary qualities do not stand or fall on its validity as a coherent system of ideas, and his works are read and appreciated by a generation which may not even have heard of the term. The conception of Unanimism gradually evolved until he transcended it; it is at this point that his work attains its greatest maturity, springing from a broad experience of life rather than the exalted but narrow insights of his youth. In some ways, Unanimism may even have been a disservice to him in deflecting his interest from the individual to the collective, when, despite the claims of the *avant-garde*, it is individual characters who in the end best hold the

168

interest both of the theater audience and the novel reader. Certainly, only after about 1918 does Romains really succeed in creating characters who are more than ciphers. Today, the collective tends to be distrusted: despite the excesses of Romantic egoism, the flowering of the individual personality is regarded as a fundamental human ideal, and in consequence Romains's early Unanimism seems regressive. And his career surely proves him one of the great individualists of the century; paradoxically, virtually every work is clearly marked with the stamp of his personality. Despite his denials, Unanimism proved an excellent method of literary advancement; equally it forms a page, if not a chapter, in literary history, and without it his work would be the poorer for lacking a valuable imaginative dimension—just as Hugo's "Chain of Being" is unacceptable as valid philosophy, although immensely fertile in his creative imagination—but its importance does not go further than this.

From Hugo, Romains also took the idea that literature ought to appeal to the widest possible public compatible with intelligent writing, and in this conviction never faltered, rejecting any narrow élitist aesthetic. And despite the shattering of his early optimism he continued to treat as his central problem the reconciliation of nineteenth century liberal ideals with the tragic realities of our age. This is the fundamental theme of *Les Hommes de Bonne Volonté,* and that his conclusions are largely pessimistic in no way diminishes this constant effort.

To Baudelaire, Romains is less indebted, and in important ways— such as the older poet's contempt for the masses—he is sharply at variance. The prime inspiration here is the quivering sensibility towards life in the modern city. In Romains we find little of Baudelaire's Satanism, but, on the other hand, in *Les Fleurs du Mal* he found a model for a volume of poetry with a distinct structure, poetry moreover which although original in inspiration required no wild innovations in form. The same is true of *La Légende des Siècles;* all Romains's collections of poetry have shown the same concern for structure, and his theory of versification, despite its apparent innovations, remains in intention determinedly classical, in the widest sense. Almost all his mature work is informed by the same respect for classical values: balance, honesty, and clarity.

The idea of the *roman-somme,* with its immense number of characters and deliberate attempt at full portrayal of society, may be traced back to Balzac, while the collective sweep of *Les Hommes de Bonne Volonté* follows directly from such novels as *Au Bonheur des Dames* and *Germinal*. This is to put Romains's fiction in the broader tradition of Realism rather than Naturalism, for although he initially shares Zola's optimism about scientific progress, he rejects any idea of the novel as objective experiment. The multivolume novel has tended to be neglected in recent years by critics in favor of experimental work where form is the major interest, but in terms of readership there can be no doubt that the *romans-fleuves* of Romains, Duhamel and Martin du Gard, let alone such later novelists as Roger Ikor or Henri Troyat, find a more receptive audience. Despite the obvious effort involved in tackling a novel spread over thousands of pages of print, the novel-series is an aesthetic legacy of the nineteenth century which we cannot discount, and Romains, the widest-ranging of French writers of his age, saw in it the sphere of his most important work. This point is worth stressing. In the nineteenth century, the verse-drama was replaced by the novel as the summit of literary achievement, and the preeminence of the novel has remained. Not without challenge: various attempts have been made, not only in France, to reestablish poetic drama; yet none has achieved more than partial success. This is precisely the situation of *Cromedeyre*: if Romains's play had encountered more than a *succès d'estime,* he might well have persevered with poetic drama instead of tackling his novel-series. Although he is read today primarily as a novelist, we should not let this single aspect of his artistic achievement overshadow his other work. As an essayist, he consistently maintains an admirable level of balanced analysis, in a style notable for its vivacity and clarity. Yet this is the part of his work least likely to survive once the topical issues which inspired them have subsided into oblivion. When *Les Hommes de Bonne Volonté* began to appear, he was considered chiefly a dramatist. The literary reputation of a playwright presents special problems, since plays in general are not much read, and work must constantly be revived in the theater if it is not to be forgotten. Yet with an ever increasing stock of plays on which to draw, revival is haphazard and arbitrary. In Romains's case, the lasting attraction of *Knock* and successful productions of several other plays have kept his name before the theater public. What in fact is his achievement in the theater? *L'Armée dans la*

Ville seems now little more than a curiosity of literary history, to be read rather than performed. It is *Cromedeyre* which, despite its lukewarm welcome, is Romains's most significant play. Its stark poetic qualities and elemental power recall, in different ways, the dramatic worlds of Synge and even Lorca, and a different staging of the play might have brought it comparable success. We can understand that Romains turned away from poetic tragedy at this point, but his later plays on the whole are, as literature, less impressive. The Le Trouhadec comedies, *Musse* and *Boën* seem distinctly slight, while *Le Dictateur,* more serious in intention, is still unsatisfactory. *Donogoo* is based on a brilliant conception and *Knock* is of course genuinely funny; its hero has climbed out of the pages of literature to become a folk hero, yet the literary qualities of the play are dubious, and its appeal largely on the *Clochemerle* level.

It is difficult to avoid the conclusion that Romains's work in the theater is ultimately only a partial success. What of his contribution as a poet? Here his work has run counter to the main poetic trends of the century in its devotion to strict prosody and clearly defined structure. When we discount the visionary rhetoric of Unanimism with its artificial emphases, we are faced by poetry of considerable force and originality. In the *Odes,* Romains attains a note of lyricism as poignant as any in the last century, while *Europe* is clearly one of the greatest works to emerge from World War I. Romains's other literary work has unfortunately obscured his reputation as a poet. Poetry is now little read by the general public, only by specialists or other poets; but while it is read at all, Romains's verse will survive. It is, however, as a novelist that Romains seems most significant. *Les Hommes de Bonne Volonté,* despite irritating flaws, remains one of the greatest novels of the century. For some critics, *Mort de quelqu'un* appears the more original, though perhaps it is better seen as simply a striking *tour de force,* which cannot really compare with the massive novel-series. Both it and *Les Copains,* a book so different, still hold a wide readership, as indeed does the *Psyché* trilogy, although this too seems to fall far short of the later series. *Nomentanus* and *Bertrand de Ganges* are attractive miniatures, but Romains's later novels are a different case and add little to his stature; it is as if with *Les Hommes de Bonne Volonté* he had virtually exhausted his fictional inspiration. Indeed, little of

Romains's production since 1946 seems likely to last, and perhaps he devoted too much attention to promoting his literary posterity. Yet ultimately an artist must be judged by his best work, not his weakest, and though Romains may fall short of the very highest literary rank, his place in the galaxy of letters is nevertheless secure.

Notes and References

Chapter One

1. *Amitiés et rencontres.* Paris, 1970, p. 7.
2. A.Bourin, *Connaissance de Jules Romains.* Paris, 1961, p. 26.
3. *La Vie Unanime.* Revised ed., Paris, 1925, p. 15.
4. E.g. M. Israël, *Jules Romains.* Paris, 1931, pp. 30–31; A. Cuisenier, *Jules Romains et l'unanimisme.* Paris, 1935, p. 17.
5. Romains in "Les Sentiments unanimes et la poésie." *Le Penseur,* April, 1905, pp. 121–24; Chennevière in "Le Frisson nouveau." *Vox,* No. 19, 1905, pp. 201–5.
6. Cf. B. Stoltzfus, *Georges Chennevière et l'unanimisme.* Paris, 1965, p. 62; R. Arbour, *Henri Bergson et les lettres françaises.* Paris, 1956, p. 242; A. Billy, *L'Époque contemporaine.* Paris, 1956, pp. 150–51.
7. *La Vie Unanime.* New ed., Paris, 1913, p. 226.
8. N. Martin-Deslias, *L'Invention divine.* Paris, 1957, p. 17.
9. *Ai-je fait ce que j'ai voulu?* Paris, 1964, p. 38.
10. W. Widdem, *Weltbejahung und Welflucht im Werke Jules Romains'.* Geneva and Paris, 1960.
11. *La Grande Revue,* 27 July 1908, p. 386; *Revue Bleue,* 4 September 1909, p. 317.
12. Jules Romains and Georges Duhamel, *Le Colloque de novembre.* Paris, 1946, p. 52.
13. B. Stoltzfus, *Georges Chennevière et l'unanimisme.* Paris, 1965, p. 39.

Chapter Two

1. *L'Âme des Hommes.* Paris, 1904, p. 1.
2. *Ibid.,* p. 3.
3. *Ibid.,* p. 25.
4. *Deux poèmes.* Paris. 1910, p. 11.
5. *Ibid.,* p. 50.
6. *Ibid.,* p. 23.
7. *Ibid.,* p. 44.
8. *Petit traité de versification.* Paris, 1923, p. 59.
9. *Ibid.,* pp. 65–69.
10. *Ibid.,* pp. 70–71.
11. *Ibid.,* p. 79.

173

12. *Ibid.*, p. 118.
13. *Le Bourg régénéré.* New ed., Paris, 1920, p. 17.
14. *Ibid.*, p. 18.
15. *La Vie Unanime.* New ed., Paris, 1925, pp. 8, 19–20.
16. *La Vie Unanime.* Paris, 1913, p. 199.
17. *Ibid.*, p. 140.
18. *Ibid.*, p. 190.
19. *Ibid.*, p. 181.
20. *Ibid.*, p. 16.
21. *Deux poèmes.* Paris, 1910, p. 53.
22. *Ibid.*, p. 57.
23. *Ibid.*, p. 59.
24. *Ibid.*, p. 60.
25. *Odes et Prières.* 5th impr., Paris, 1923, p. 125.
26. *Ai-je fait ce que j'ai voulu?* Paris, 1964, p. 49.
27. *Manuel de Déification.* Paris, 1910. pp. 17–18.
28. *Ibid.*, pp. 18–19.
29. *Ibid.*, p. 23.
30. *Ibid.*, pp. 40–41.
31. *Ibid.*, p. 48.
32. *Ibid.*, p. 62.
33. *Un Être en marche.* Paris, 1910, p. 22.
34. *Ibid.*, p. 26.
35. *Ibid.*, p. 116.
36. *L'Armée dans la Ville.* Paris, 1911, p. x.
37. Cf. P. J. Norrish, *The Drama of the Group.* Cambridge, 1958, p. 58.
38. There was considerable interest in Hebbel about this time in France, several books on him appearing between 1907 and 1911. A French translation of *Judith,* by Gaston Gallimard and Pierre de Lanux, came out in November, 1911; Romains mentions this later in his career (*Problèmes européens,* Paris, 1933, p. 36) and may indeed have known it before publication. Another *Judith,* by Giraudoux, was staged by Jouvet in 1931, but proved a failure.
39. *La Nouvelle Revue Française,* April, 1912, p. 612.
40. *Ai-je fait ce que j'ai voulu?* Paris, 1964, p. 55.
41. *Odes et Prières.* 5th impr., Paris, 1923, p. 46.
42. *Ibid.*, p. 52.
43. *Ibid.*, p. 54.
44. A. Cuisenier, *L'Art de Jules Romains.* Paris, 1949, p. 211.
45. *Mort de quelqu'un.* Paris, 1933, p. 56.
46. *Ai-je fait ce que j'ai voulu?* Paris, 1964, p. 56.
47. *Puissances de Paris.* Paris, 1911, p. 172.
48. *Ibid.*, p. 180.

49. *Ai-je fait ce que j'ai voulu?* Paris, 1964, p. 178; A. Cuisenier, *L'Art de Jules Romains.* Paris, 1949, p. 218.

50. *Les Copains.* 140th impr., Paris, 1947, pp. 231–32.

51. *Ibid.,* pp. 233–34.

52. *Les Bonnes Feuilles,* XXIV. Paris: Librairie du Travail, 1925.

53. *Ai-je fait ce que j'ai voulu?* Paris, 1964, p. 101; M. Israël, *Jules Romains.* Paris, 1931, p. 248.

54. *Le Voyage des amants.* Paris, 1920, p. 9.

55. *Ibid.,* p. 27.

56. *Ai-je fait ce que j'ai voulu?* Paris, 1964, pp. 101-2.

Chapter Three

1. *Chants des dix années.* Paris, 1928, p. 12.

2. *Ibid.,* pp. 29–30.

3. *Ibid.,* p. 45.

4. *Ibid.,* p. 94.

5. Leïla Holterhoff Heyn and René Maublanc, *Une éducation paroptique: La découverte du monde visuel par un aveugle.* Paris: N.R.F., 1926. Maublanc was to become a close member of Romains's circle, writing a number of critical articles on his work.

6. *Eyeless Sight.* London, 1924, p. 201 (this translation contains a postface by Romains).

7. G. Duhamel, *Les Espoirs et les épreuves.* Paris, 1953, pp. 76–78.

8. *Théâtre,* III. Paris, 1926. p. 71.

9. A. Bourin, *Connaissance de Jules Romains.* Paris, 1961, p. 45.

10. *Théâtre,* III. Paris, 1926, pp. 98 & 107.

11. "Pourquoi j'ai écrit Donogoo." *Revue de Paris,* November, 1951, pp. 3–4.

12. Cf. P. Léautaud, *Journal littéraire,* IV. Paris 1957, pp. 138–43; *Le Théâtre de Maurice Boissard,* II. Paris, 1926, pp. 299–307.

13. *Amitiés et rencontres.* Paris, 1970, p. 38.

14. M. E. Coindreau, *La Farce est jouée.* New York, 1942, p. 232.

15. L. Jouvet, *Témoignages sur le théâtre.* Paris, 1952, pp. 103–4. Romains's *Amédée* should not be confused with Ionesco's play of 1954, *Amédée ou comment s'en débarrasser?*

16. The date of the first production of *Démétrios* is given in *Théâtre,* IV. Paris, 1926, as 9 October 1926. This is an error for 9 October 1925, when *Démétrios* was put on with Charles Vildrac's *Madame Béliard.* Cf. B. L. Knapp, *Louis Jouvet: Man of the Theater.* New York, 1957, pp. 102 & 277.

17. A not very perceptive review of *Le Dieu des corps* by René Maublanc in *Europe,* December, 1928, (pp. 569–74), was followed by a long letter by Romains correcting some of Maublanc's misapprehensions (pp. 575–78).

18. *Chants des dix années.* Paris, 1928, pp. 105–6.
19. *Ai-je fait ce que j'ai voulu?* Paris, 1964, p. 102.
20. *Chants des dix années.* Paris, 1928, p. 130.
21. *Ibid.,* p. 132.
21. *Ibid.,* p. 134.
23. *Ibid.,* p. 152.

Chapter Four

1. *L'Homme blanc.* Paris, 1937, p. 36.
2. *Ibid.,* p. 28.
3. *Ibid.,* p. 25.
4. *Ibid.,* p. 65.
5. *Ibid.,* p. 86.
6. *Ibid.,* p. 127.
7. *Pour l'esprit et la liberté.* Paris, 1937, pp. 22.
8. *Une Vue des choses.* New York, 1941, p. 30.
9. *Ibid.,* p. 35.
10. *Pierres levées.* Mexico City, 1945, p. 16.
11. *Ibid.,* p. 62.

Chapter Five

1. *Les Hommes de Bonne Volonté,* I. Paris, 1932, p. v. We should note, however, that Romains himself disliked the term *roman-fleuve.*
2. *Ibid.,* p. xi.
3. *Ibid.,* p. xvi.
4. *Amitiés et rencontres.* Paris, 1970, p. 130.
5. A special volume entitled *Paris des Hommes de Bonne Volonté,* edited by Lise Jules-Romains, was published, with maps of different districts of Paris showing exactly where many episodes in the novel took place.
6. In *Cahiers des Hommes de Bonne Volonté,* IV. Paris, 1950, pp. 39–49; reprinted in *Amitiés et rencontres.* Paris, 1970. There is also a Quinette, a glove merchant, in Zola's *Au Bonheur des Dames.*
7. A. Bourin, *Connaissance de Jules Romains.* Paris, 1961, p. 122.
8. There is a hint of this in Gabrielle Romains, *Geneviève retrouvée.* Paris, 1962, p. 71.
9. A. Bourin, *Connaissance de Jules Romains.* Paris, 1961, p. 161.
10. Romains discusses his attitude to the Académie Française in Bourin, pp. 226–30. He claims that he was approached by the Perpetual Secretary as early as 1931, but consistently refused to become a candidate until 1945, when the situation had been radically transformed and when de Gaulle himself appealed to him to stand. He also describes reading his pages on

Allory's candidacy to Roger Martin du Gard in 1936; Martin du Gard, however, who evidently knew his man, offered to bet that Romains would be the first of the two to weaken and join the Immortals. Romains does not tell us if he accepted the wager.

11. In particular, a friend and colleague from Laon, Albert Cazes, served at Verdun and could pass on detailed accounts of the events there (M. Berry, *Jules Romains, sa vie, son œuvre*. Paris, 1953, p. 76).

12. *Les Hauts et les bas de la liberté*. Paris, 1960, p. 64.

13. Romains may have used information from Luc Durtain, one of the Abbaye group, who traveled to Russia about 1923, publishing a book, *La Source rouge,* in 1924.

14. Reprinted in *Saints de notre calendrier*. Paris, 1952, pp. 213–27.

Chapter Six

1. *Ai-je fait ce que j'ai voulu?* Paris, 1964, p. 156.

2. *Maisons*. Paris, 1953, p. XLVII.

3. *Ibid.,* p. XXXIX.

4. *Ai-je fait ce que j'ai voulu?* Paris, 1964, p. 159.

5. *Un grand honnête homme*. London, Harrap, 1963, pp. 34–36.

6. Cf. *Lettres à un ami,* I. Paris, 1964, p. 187, where Romains replies to Mauriac's article in *Le Figaro Littéraire,* 28 October 1961.

Selected Bibliography

During his career Romains wrote many hundreds of articles as well as books. All the latter are listed, together with English translations where available, but owing to the ephemeral nature of the former, only those referred to in the text or otherwise unusually important have been recorded. The date of first publication is normally given; certain of Romains's works have reappeared later, sometimes under a different imprint. Where works have been republished under a different title, this is indicated.

There is by now a considerable amount of critical literature on Romains of widely varying value. Only work published in book form is included, and the list of titles given is sharply selective. Fuller bibliographies are given in M. Berry, *Jules Romains, sa vie, son œuvre*. Paris, 1953 and P. J. Norrish, *The Drama of the Group*. Cambridge, 1958.

Place of publication is Paris unless otherwise stated.

PRIMARY SOURCES

1. Works by Romains

a) *Poetry and Unanimist Theory*

L'Âme des Hommes. Société des Poètes Français, 1904.

"Les Sentiments unanimes et la Poésie." *Le Penseur,* April, 1905, pp. 121–24.

"Aux hommes de mon age." *Revue Littéraire de Paris de Champagne,* April, 1906, pp. 279–83.

"Projet concernant la poésie." *La Phalange,* 15 December 1907, pp. 542–45.

La Vie Unanime. L'Abbaye, 1908. Further editions were brought out by the Mercure de France in 1913, and with an important preface by Romains, by the N.R.F. in 1925.

"À propos de l'Unanimisme." *La Grande Revue*, 25 July 1908, pp. 386–95.

À la Foule qui est ici. Impr. du XXe siècle, 1909.

Premier livre de Prières. Vers et Prose, 1909.

Deux Poèmes. Mercure de France, 1910. Contains *Le Poème du Métropolitain* and *Ode à la Foule qui est ici*.

Manuel de Déification. Sansot, 1910.

Un Être en marche. Mercure de France, 1910.

Odes et Prières. Mercure de France, 1913. Includes *Odes, Premier livre de Prières,* and *Ode à la Foule qui est ici*.

Europe. N.R.F., 1916.

Les Quatre Saisons. Monnier, 1917.

Le Voyage des amants. N.R.F., 1920.

Amour couleur de Paris. N.R.F., 1921.

Petit traité de versification (with G. Chennevière). N.R.F., 1923.

Ode Génoise. Bloch, 1925.

Chants des dix années. N.R.F., 1928. Contains *Europe, Amour couleur de Paris* and *Ode Génoise.*

L'Homme blanc. Flammarion, 1937.

Choix de poèmes. Gallimard, 1948. A selection by Romains, containing three hitherto unpublished *Complaintes.*

Pierres levées. Flammarion, 1948.

Maisons. Seghers, 1953.

b) *Fiction*

"Le Rassemblement." *Le Penseur,* June, 1905, pp. 225–29.

Le Bourg régénéré. Vanier, Messein, 1906.

Mort de quelqu'un. Figuière, 1911.

Puissances de Paris. Figuière, 1911.

Les Copains. Figuière, 1913.

Sur les Quais de la Villette. Figuière, 1914. Reprinted as *Le Vin blanc de La Villette.* N.R.F., 1923.

Lucienne. N.R.F., 1922.

Le Dieu des Corps. N.R.F., 1928.

Quand le navire . . . . N.R.F., 1929.

Les Hommes de Bonne Volonté. 27 volumes. Flammarion, 1932–1946.

Nomentanus le réfugié. New York, Editions de la Maison Francaise, 1943.

Tu ne tueras point. In *Les Dix Commandements.* New York, Editions de la Maison Française, 1944.

Bertrand de Ganges. New York, Éditions de la Maison Française, 1944.

Le Moulin et l'hospice. Flammarion, 1949.

Docteur Knock: Fragments de la Doctrine Secrète. Bruker, 1949.

Lettre à A. O. Barnabooth. Liège, Éditions Dynamo, 1950.

Violation de frontières. Flammarion, 1951.

Interviews avec Dieu, by "John W. Hicks." Flammarion, 1952.

Le Fils de Jerphanion. Flammarion, 1956.

Une femme singulière. Flammarion, 1957.

Le Besoin de voir clair. Flammarion, 1958.

Mémoires de Madame Chauverel, I. Flammarion, 1959.

Mémoires de Madame Chauverel, II. Flammarion, 1960.

Un grand honnête homme. Flammarion, 1961.

Portraits d'inconnus. Flammarion, 1962.

c) *Drama*

L'Armée dans la Ville. Mercure de France, 1911.

Cromedeyre-le-Vieil. N.R.F., 1920.

Donogoo-Tonka, ou les Miracles de la Science. N.R.F., 1920.

Monsieur le Trouhadec saisi par la Débauche. N.R.F., 1921.

Théâtre I. N.R.F., 1924. Contains *Knock* and *M. Le Trouhadec saisi par la Débauche.*

Théâtre II. N.R.F., 1925. Contains *Le Mariage de Le Trouhadec* and *La Scintillante.*

Théâtre III. N.R.F., 1926. Contains *Cromedeyre-le-Vieil* and *Amédée.*

Théâtre IV. N.R.F., 1926. Contains *Le Dictateur* and *Démétrios.*

Jean le Maufranc. L'Illustration, 1927.

Théâtre V. N.R.F., 1929. Contains *Volpone* and *Le Déjeuner marocain.*

Théâtre VI. N.R.F., 1929. Contains *Jean le Maufranc* and *Musse.*

Donogoo. L'Illustration, 1931.

Boën, ou la Possession des biens. L'Illustration, 1931.

Le Roi masqué. Fayard, 1932.

Théâtre VII. N.R.F., 1935. Contains *Boën* and *Donogoo.*

L'An Mil. Éditions de l'Odéon, 1947.

"Pourquoi j'ai écrit *Donogoo*," *Revue de Paris,* November, 1951, pp. 3–7.

Barbazouk. Les Œuvres Libres, No. 209 (October, 1963), pp. 159–262.

d) *Essays*

La Vision extra-rétinienne et le Sens paroptique, by Louis Farigoule. N.R.F., 1920.

Preface to B. Mahn, *Souvenirs du Vieux Colombier.* Aveline, 1926.

La Vérité en bouteilles. Trémois, 1927.

Problèmes européens. Flammarion, 1933.

Le Couple France-Allemagne. Flammarion, 1934.

Zola et son exemple. Flammarion, 1935.

Visite aux Américains. Flammarion, 1936.

Pour l'esprit et la liberté. N.R.F., 1937.

Cela dépend de vous. Flammarion, 1938.

"Ce qu'un écrivain pense de la situation." Speech made to the American Club in Paris, 11 April 1940.

Sept Mystères du Destin de l'Europe. New York: Éditions de la Maison Française, 1940.

Messages aux Français. New York: Éditions de la Maison Française, 1941.

Stefan Zweig, grand Européen. New York: Éditions de la Maison Française, 1941.

Une Vue des choses. New York: Éditions de la Maison Française, 1941.

Mission ou demission de la France? Mexico City: Quetzal, 1942.

Salsette découvre l'Amérique. New York: Éditions de la Maison Française, 1942.

Actualité de Victor Hugo. Mexico City: Librairie Française, 1944.

Retrouver la foi. New York: Éditions de la Maison Française, 1944.

Le Colloque de novembre. Flammarion, 1946. Romains's speech on his

reception into the Académie Française, with Georges Duhamel's reply.
Le Probleme N⁰ 1. Plon, 1947.
Saints de notre calendrier. Flammarion, 1952.
Confidences d'un auteur dramatique. Estienne, 1953.
Examen de conscience des Français. Flammarion, 1954.
Passagers de cette planète, où allons-nous? Grasset, 1955.
Preface to N. Martin-Deslias, *L'Invention divine.* La Colombe, 1957.
Souvenirs et confidences d'un écrivain. Fayard, 1958. Includes *Confidences
    d'un auteur dramatique.*
Situation de la terre. Flammarion, 1958.
Cinquantenaire du 6 octobre. Flammarion, 1958.
Hommes, Médecins, Machines. Flammarion, 1959.
Pour raison garder, I. Flammarion, 1960.
Les Hauts et les bas de la liberté. Flammarion, 1960. Includes *Messages aux
    Français, Mission ou démission de la France,* and *Retrouver la foi.*
Connaissance de Jules Romains. Flammarion, 1961. This study by André
    Bourin contains detailed commentaries by Romains.
Landowski: La Main et l'Esprit. Bibliothèque des Arts, 1961.
Contribution to *Alexandre le Grand.* Hachette, 1962.
Napoléon par lui-même. Librarie Académique Perrin, 1963.
Pour raison garder, II. Flammarion, 1963.
Ai-je fait ce que j'ai voulu? Wesmaël-Charlier, 1964.
Lettres à un ami, I. Flammarion, 1964.
Lettres à un ami, II. Flammarion, 1965.
Lettre ouverte contre une vaste conspiration. Albin Michel, 1966.
Pour raison garder, III. Flammarion, 1967.
Marc-Aurèle, ou l'Empereur de bonne volonté. Flammarion, 1968.
Amitiés et rencontres. Flammarion, 1970.

2. *English Translations*

Mort de quelqu'un: Death of a Nobody. New York: Huebsch, 1914.
Les Copains: The Boys in the Back Room. New York: McBride, 1937.
La Vision extra-rétinienne: Eyeless Sight. New York, Putnam, 1924.
Knock: Dr. Knock. London: Benn, 1925.
Lucienne, Le Dieu des Corps, Quand le navire . . . : The Body's Rapture.
    New York: Liveright, 1933.
Les Hommes de Bonne Volonté: Men of Good Will. New York: Knopf,
    1933–1946.
Sept Mystères du Destin de l'Europe: The Seven Mysteries of Europe. New
    York: Knopf, 1940.
Stefan Zweig, grand Européen: Stefan Zweig: Great European. New
    York: Viking Press, 1941.

Salsette découvre l'Amérique: Salsette Discovers America. New York: Knopf, 1942.

Tu ne tueras point: Thou Shalt Not Kill. In *The Ten Commandments.* New York: Simon and Schuster, 1943.

Violation de frontières: Tussles with Time. London: Sidgwick & Jackson, 1952.

Examen de conscience des Français: A Frenchman Examines His Conscience. London: Deutsch, 1955.

Une femme singulière: The Adventuress. London: Muller, 1958.

Situation de la terre: As It Is On Earth. New York: Macmillan, 1962.

Lettre ouverte contre une vaste conspiration: Open Letter Against a Vast Conspiracy. New York: Heineman, 1967.

SECONDARY SOURCES

1. The following are entirely devoted to articles on Romains:

Hommage à Jules Romains. Le Mouton Blanc, September-October, 1923.

Hommage à Jules Romains. Les Cahiers de Paris, January, 1939.

Hommage à Jules Romains pour son 60ᵉ anniversaire. Flammarion, 1945.

Les Cahiers des Hommes de Bonne Volonté:

   I.   *La Notion d'Homme de Bonne Volonté.* Flammarion, 1948.

   II.   *L'Amitié.* Flammarion, 1948.

   III. *Où va le monde?* Flammarion, 1949.

   IV. *Le Crime.* Flammarion, 1950.

Les Nouvelles Littéraires, 26 August 1965, pp. 1, 6–8, also contains a number of articles in homage to Romains on his eightieth birthday.

2. *Critical Works*

BERRY, M., *Jules Romains, sa vie, son œuvre.* Le Conquistador, 1953.

———, *Jules Romains.* Éditions Universitaires, 1959.

    Useful summaries of Romains's career and work.

BIDAL, M. L., *Les Écrivains de l'Abbaye.* Boivin, 1938. A sensible study of the Abbaye group of poets, together with Romains and Chennevière.

BLASER, H., *De l'influence alternée et simultanée des éléments sensibles et intellectuels dans les œuvres de Jules Romains.* Zurich: Lang, 1941. A doctoral thesis containing valuable critical insights into Romains's work

CUISENIER, A., *Jules Romains et l'unanimisme.* Flammarion, 1935.

———, *L'Art de Jules Romains.* Flammarion, 1949.

———, *Jules Romains et les Hommes de Bonne Volonté.* Flammarion, 1954.

    The most solid critical studies of Romains, by a friend from student days.

DÉCAUDIN, M., *La Crise des valeurs symbolistes.* Toulouse: Privat, 1960.

    An exhaustive account of French poetry in the years from 1895 to 1914.

FIGUERAS, A., *Jules Romains.* Seghers, 1952. An enthusiastic outline of Romains's poetry in the series *Poètes d'aujourd'hui.*

GUISAN, G., *Poésie et collectivité.* Lausanne: Éditions des Trois Collines, Paris: Monier, 1938. A sensitive study of Romains, Chennevière, and the Abbaye poets.

ISRAËL, M., *Jules Romains, sa vie, son œuvre.* Kra, 1931. Apparently the same author as M. Berry.

MARTIN-DESLIAS, N., *Jules Romains ou Quand les Hommes de Bonne Volonté se cherchent.* Nagel, 1951. Intelligent comments on Romains's novel-series.

NORRISH, P. J., *Drama of the Group.* Cambridge University Press, 1958. A valuable analysis of Unanimism in relation to Romains's drama.

PFEIFFER, R., *Les Hommes de Bonne Volonté von Jules Romains.* Winterthur: Keller, 1958. A careful study of Romains's novel-series containing many insights.

SPITZER, L., *Stilstudien,* II, Munich: Hueber, 1961. Includes a brilliant analysis of Romains's early style.

STOLZFUS, B., *Georges Chennevière et l'unanimisme.* Minard, 1965. Contains many sensible reflections on Romains and Unanimism.

WIDDEM, W., *Weltbejahung und Weltflucht im Werke Jules Romains'.* Geneva: Droz, Paris: Minard, 1960. Identifies two important contradictory tendencies in Romains's work.

Index

185